Acoustics in buildings

Bernard Gréhant

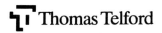

Thomas Telford

Published by Thomas Telford Publishing, Thomas Telford Services Ltd, 1 Heron Quay, London E14 4JD

First published in French as 'Acoustique et bâtiment' in 1994 by Lavoisier Tec & Doc, Paris
First published in English 1996

Distributors for Thomas Telford books are
USA: American Society of Civil Engineers, Publications Sales Department, 345 East 47th Street, New York, NY 10017–2398
Japan: Maruzen Co. Ltd, Book Department, 3–10 Nihonbashi 2-chome, Chuo-ku, Tokyo 103
Australia: DA Books and Journals, 648 Whitehorse Road, Mitcham 3132, Victoria

A catalogue record for this book is available from the British Library

Classification
Availability: Unrestricted
Content: Guidance based on best current practice
Status: Author's opinion
User: Civil, structural and acoustics engineers, architects and engineering designers

ISBN: 0 7277 2511 4

Typeset by Tradespools Limited, Frome, Somerset
Printed in Great Britain by The Cromwell Press, Melksham, Wilts.

Foreword

All who work in industry, whether manufacturing, assembling, installing or selling equipment, are constantly being required to offer clients much quieter products.

For several decades now, the battle against noise has been part of our effort to protect the environment. The first targets were noise from airports, road traffic and the workplace, but soon noise from within buildings, whether from domestic appliances such as vacuum cleaners and washing machines, or from structural appliances such as lifts, boilers and motorized blinds and shutters, became the subject of legislation.

Regulations are now appearing which follow the same route. However, we have had to anticipate the legislation, largely as a result of customer requirements which have, justifiably, become as demanding of building services products as of cars.

For the past two years, SOMFY has been engaged in a research programme with the Centre for Building Science and Technology (CSTB–Centre Scientifique et Technique du Bâtiment) in Grenoble to establish the best methods of controlling the many separate and interactive acoustic excitation effects in the structure of a building. This research is intended to complement previous work which focused only on the company's own products.

This research has benefited from the combined support of the Construction and Architecture Planning Department of the French Ministry of Housing and the Environment and Energy Control Agency.

We have asked Bernard Gréhant to present the results,

without restriction. We believe it important to give our industrial customers, installers, specifiers and (once in a while does no harm!) fellow manufacturers the benefit of all those elements which contribute, in the interest of all, to making the various living environments designed by our architects as pleasing to the ears as they are to the eyes.

Paul Dreyfus
Chairman, SOMFY International

Preface

Noise is one of the major plagues of modern life. In severe cases it poses a threat to physiological health; but its potential for threatening psychological well-being, which can lead to the disruption of social relationships, is more insidious. Its adverse effects are widespread among the inhabitants of crowded urban communities. However, if you suffer from noise in the workplace and in the streets, you can always retreat to your home and shut out the hubbub of the world outside—or so you would think. But no! The very building which is supposed to afford you much needed protection is alive with the sound of motors, fans, pumps, valves, doors and a variety of other sources of acoustic disturbance.

Bernard Gréhant has combined a technical knowledge developed in the academic world with his extensive experience of working for many years to suppress the noise and vibration generated by the products of SOMFY International, to produce a book which explains, in easily accessible form, and through many practical examples, the nature of noise generation by machinery in buildings, together with techniques for its reduction by means of appropriate mechanical design.

Although this book concentrates on a specific range of SOMFY products (solar protection and motorized shutting systems), the general principles and methods of noise and vibration control applied to these products have widespread application. Design and installation engineers will appreciate the down-to-earth style of the presentation which emphasizes the physical understanding of the mechanisms which generate and propagate sound as the prerequisite for success.

I congratulate the author and SOMFY for sharing the fruits of their endeavours in a frank and illuminating manner, and I welcome this publication as a valuable contribution to the fight against the ubiquitous foe of tranquillity and rest.

Professor F. J. Fahy
8 March 1996

Acknowledgements

Special thanks are due to Michel Villot and Claude Martin, acoustic engineers, CSTB Grenoble and to Professor F. J. Fahy, Institute of Sound and Vibration Research, University of Southampton.

Highly aware of the importance of improvements in living conditions in housing, the Construction and Architecture Planning Department of the French Ministry of Housing and the Environment and Energy Control Agency have assisted part of the studies described in this book.

Directed by Jacques Roland, the team of the Sound Laboratory of the Centre Scientifique et Technique du Bâtiment (CSTB) in Grenoble has contributed greatly in supplying experimental material and theoretical analysis resulting in many observations, discussions and recommendations that appear in Parts Two and Three of this book. Michel Villot and Claude Martin deserve special mention for their personal investment in these studies, also for reading and improving parts of the French book. Also given in one of the chapters, devoted to motor-reducers, are findings and observations from research work conducted at the Vibrations and Sound Laboratory of INSA at Lyon by B. Guerin and L. Bouchard, supervised by Professor C. Lesueur.

Among equipment manufacturers there is ever-growing concern regarding the need for knowledge and competence regarding the vibration and acoustic behaviour of their products. We thank SOMFY's customer companies for their many contributions to the studies presented and to others still under way on the same topic.

SOMFY intends to be one of the pacesetters of this movement. This book consequently owes much to the contributions by C. Viste, G. Charnay, A. Baud and O. Jacquet who, within the company, incorporate acoustic considerations in design, testing methods, specification of accessories and organization of field tests.

We thank also the companies Bruel & Kjaer and 01dB and the Centre d'information et de Documentation sur le Bruit (CIDB) which have given permission to illustrate the text with some very welcome photographs.

Thanks also to Nicholas Flay, who translated this book and, last but not least, we want to express our gratitude to Professor Frank J. Fahy, who accepted the task of prefacing it, despite a sometimes too pragmatic approach and a lot of remaining defects which did not escape the vigilance for which he is well known.

Introduction

Noise produced by heavy motorized equipment installed in buildings (such as lifts, ventilation, heating and air conditioning plant) has for several years been prompting research, regulations and comprehensive, well presented specialist works.

The increasing motorization of light installations can meet new requirements for comfort, safety and energy conservation by active control of the building shell. Most often this motorization has simply involved attaching an electric motor to a device that traditionally was manually operated. In terms of vibrations, however, the behaviour in the two cases is radically different.

It occurred to us that the specific problems associated with noise reduction in light motorized equipment in buildings merited presentation as a book, for the instruction of industrial designers and architects. This book is therefore intended for readers with a technical, but not necessarily scientific, background. It addresses architects and building specifiers but equally installers needing more information than is usually given in catalogues. It should also be useful for lecturers who wish to illustrate their courses with concrete examples from the worlds of industry or building construction—and, of course, their students. The challenge was how to go about writing it.

Noise is a phenomenon that can be irritating and even traumatizing. Each one of us has at least once in our lives suffered from noise and its most unpleasant effects and is clearly aware of what lies behind the word 'noisy'.

However, noise can become even more exasperating—when it

comes to studying it in order to combat it more effectively. Too often the scientific and technical literature discourages the reader with the complexity of the phenomena and the mathematical paraphernalia needed. The quantitative description of a noise source alone requires a certain level of expertise. Add to that the biological, psychological and the medical aspects: how do we avoid giving up?

And yet, behind the real complexity of causes and effects is hidden a surprising truth: like a mythological god, Noise is merciless to the designer who refuses to grant it the few sacrifices it demands. Conversely, it can be generous and discreet, provided that the rules it lays down are scrupulously respected. Paradoxically there are few rules and they are relatively straightforward. We are going to discover them.

A great mixer of sounds and meeting point of disciplines, Noise also brings people together: cooperation is an indispensable component of any action in this field. The theme of this book will provide an excellent illustration.

A firm designs, makes and distributes tubular motors. These are incorporated into equipment for buildings (roller shutters, blinds, screens and so on) designed and produced by another company. The product is then installed as a unit in a structure, thought up by an architect and built by people from a wide range of trades.

A motorized unit linked to a building: at least three distinct components working towards the same end. Are there three independent questions here? Or do the questions involved relate to one component? There is in fact just one question, a collective responsibility: it is an area where interactions are extremely strong. The efforts of one of the components can prove to be in vain if not matched by the work of the others. In return, the potential benefits are considerable.

This is the essence of what we are attempting to show, in a book conceived with the intention of tackling all the phenomena essential for understanding noise, its causes and the means of dealing with it. Wherever possible, however, the theoretical aspects are simplified: only the inevitable logarithm will make a few appearances to justify its presence alongside the decibels that numerous exercises will teach us to master.

The first chapters can easily be skipped by the specialist acquainted with acoustics and vibrations, who can concentrate on the main body of the book, which details and comments on the results of research conducted with the highly effective cooperation of the experimental centre INSA at Lyon, and of the Building Science and Technology Centre (CSTB) at Grenoble. The specialist will then be at leisure, on a second perusal, to judge the value of the simplified presentation which, we hope, the readers for whom it is intended will find attractive.

Bernard Gréhant

Contents

Part one The tools

1

Vibrations

Oscillatory movement

The classic example of the spring, supporting a mass M, which is then shifted away from its equilibrium position, gives an excellent illustration of a natural oscillatory movement (Fig. 1.1).

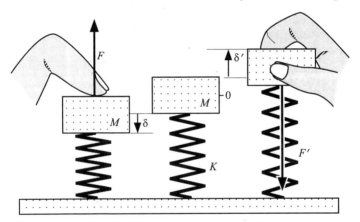

Fig. 1.1   Mass, spring and restoring force

Owing to its own weight, the mass first compresses the spring, which will reach a new state of equilibrium. We are going to focus only on the displacements which occur after this on either side of this equilibrium position, marked by position 0.

Whether compressed or stretched, the spring exerts on the mass a return force F, which immediately brings it back to 0 if it is not kept in this 'non-equilibrium' position.

This force is proportional to the elongation. The coefficient that expresses this proportionality is designated by the stiffness K of the spring. Stiffness is a parameter characteristic of every spring, dependent on its material and geometry. For a given force, elongation δ is smaller the greater the stiffness

$$\delta = -\frac{F}{K}$$

The minus sign indicates that the force is opposite to the displacement. If the elongation is negative (under compression), the force tends to produce an extension. If δ is positive, the force tends to contract the spring.

'A spring does not like changes in length'

Once the whole mass-spring unit has been moved far from 0, we free the mass, then confronted with the force F produced by the spring.

A fundamental relationship in dynamics established by Newton in the eighteenth century, and moreover everyday experience, shows that M undergoes an acceleration γ proportional to the applied force and inversely proportional to M

$$\gamma = \frac{F}{M}$$

The higher the mass, the smaller the acceleration.

'Mass does not like changes in velocity'

There you have the reason why the combination of these two uncompromising characters, the mass and the spring, give such interesting effects.

What is the next step? Submitted to F, M starts off on a movement towards the point of equilibrium. The force and the acceleration diminish progressively when M approaches this position, but the velocity continues to increase: it is only at the brief passage through 0 that the acceleration is cancelled out. However, once M has gathered velocity, it can do nothing other than keep going (which conveys, for the same reasons, the unwillingness of a mass body to stop once in motion).

The mass progressively compresses the spring, which then exerts a force opposite to the motion, the greater the force the stronger the compression, that gradually slows down the movement of M. The mass therefore stops (t_3), only to start off again immediately in the other direction, under the spring's action, in the direction of this unattainable position of rest.

This permanent exchange of energy between the mass and the spring will therefore give rise to an oscillatory motion which, if it were not for friction, would last until the end of time.

Figure 1.2 shows the changing position of the mass with time, by a periodic motion. In this example it is repeated every 0·25 s, the time for one elementary cycle called period T of the movement. Consequently $T = 0·25$ s (per cycle).

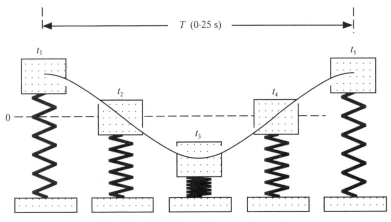

Fig. 1.2 Oscillation of mass-spring system

The number of cycles per unit time is inversely proportional to the period and constitutes the frequency f of the movement

$$f = \frac{1}{T}$$

The frequency is expressed in inverse seconds (second)$^{-1}$ or hertz (Hz). To take an example, $1/0{\cdot}25 = 4$ (cycles per second) $= 4\,Hz$. The variation around the position of equilibrium is said to be alternating: sometimes positive, sometimes negative in relation to the equilibrium position. The average variation is zero. The maximum value it takes is the amplitude of the motion, here equal to the initial displacement of the mass. In Fig. 1.3, using different units, are represented the displacement δ, the velocity v and the return force exerted by the spring on the mass.

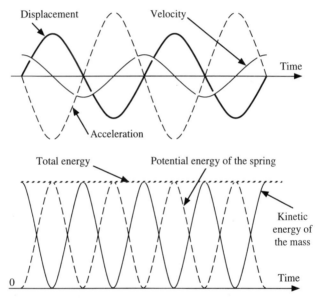

Fig. 1.3 γ (or F), δ, σ and energy values plotted against time

It is worth observing and comparing how these quantities develop with time. In particular note the behaviour of two of the quantities when the third is zero, or conversely when it reaches its maximum. The oscillation frequency depends on the mass and on the stiffness of the spring: it is higher for greater stiffnesses and smaller masses. This frequency is termed natural frequency of oscillation f_n, to distinguish it from the forced frequency which the system takes on when we want to control it rather than let it develop in its own way.

$$f_n = \left(\frac{1}{2\pi}\right)\sqrt{\frac{K}{M}}$$

The kinetic energy of the mass is proportional to the square of its velocity. Similarly, the spring's potential energy is proportional to the square of its elongation. The time-course of these two quantities is also presented in Fig. 1.3, using the same time-scale, which allows comparison with the velocity and the displacement. The sum of these two values is constant, which clearly expresses the continual transfer of energy from one to the other and the absence of any dissipation by friction. This constant value here represents the energy which had to be supplied to the system initially, to move it away from its equilibrium position.

The sinusoid: a step towards harmony

The oscillatory movement just described is sinusoidal. It is the most natural, regular, indeed the most 'comfortable' of alternating movements.

To be convinced, let us imagine that we put ourselves inside a moving body propelled by an alternating movement, and that we have to choose between several alternating movements of different speed, but with the same amplitude and frequency. The recordings shown in Fig. 1.4 give the time course of the position of the body in motion.

Apparently the simplest alternating motion by appearance is a long period of rest either side of the equilibrium position. All goes well until the balance is lost, the speed with which the position changes requires an abrupt increase in velocity and therefore a huge acceleration. The best trained astronauts would not be able to withstand it.

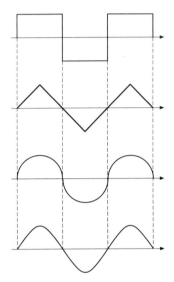

Fig. 1.4   Which is the most natural movement?

Already more acceptable, the 'triangular' alternating movement involves a constant velocity in one direction, up to a
maximum position, then a constant velocity in the opposite
direction. However, this sudden change in the velocity direction,
at the instant of rebound, also implies an acceleration which is,
in principle, infinite.

In the end, the specifications for a 'comfortable' alternating
movement are easy to define. Because it consists of going from
one extreme to the other and return in a given time (period), it is
better to achieve it with gradual, limited changes in acceleration,
and therefore gradual, limited changes in velocity.

The third test is not completely satisfactory, as the movement
becomes infinitely too fast when it passes through the median
position.

The sinusoidal displacement is the winner. If we return to Fig.
1.3, which gives the time-course of displacement, velocity and
acceleration, we observe a remarkable property: a sinusoidal

motion brings with it a velocity that is also sinusoidal, but shifted by a quarter of a period. The velocity reaches zero when the displacement is at a maximum. Conversely, the velocity is maximum when the body crosses the equilibrium position.

This new curve, which accompanies the preceding one so well is called cosinusoid. And the acceleration, which is nothing other than the velocity of the development of the velocity, also follows a sinusoidal path, one quarter of a period out of phase with the preceding quantity. Values of displacement and acceleration are consequently opposite at a given instant.

So the sinusoid seems to have the advantage, but who could state positively that it would beat other contenders? The ancient Greek scholars decreed that there is no periodic movement more beautiful than that of a moving body describing a circular trajectory at constant velocity. And the Greeks certainly knew about beauty.

For an observer watching the movement, not from the front but in profile, this displacement appears linear, alternating and, indeed, sinusoidal. Sine and cosine correspond to the projections of a radius of the circle in two directions, perpendicular to one another (Fig. 1.5(a)).

To recognize the qualities of a uniform circular movement in a plane it is essential to know the qualities of a sinusoidal law for a rectilinear alternating motion.

A turn on the big wheel at the fair (Fig. 1.5) will provide a change of scene before going any further. Fig. 1.5(b) shows the wheel at a given instant t_0, and alongside the altitude of car attachment points in the course of time. Car 3 moves a quarter of a period later than car 1. In terms of angle, the difference is 90° out of phase with car 1. Car 7 can be seen as having either a 270° lag, or as 90° ahead of car 1.

Figure 1.5(c) shows a false manoeuvre which gives us the chance to see what happens at a higher frequency. The respective amplitude and phase displacement are maintained, but some over-sensitive passengers express serious reservations about the quality of the movement.

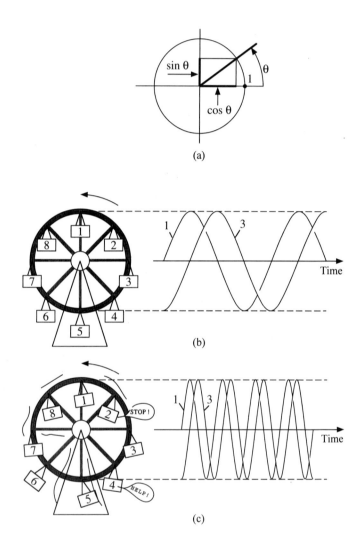

Fig. 1.5   Projections of a circular motion

Spectral analysis

Most mechanical systems show enough good form to have a sinusoidal behaviour when they oscillate with a low amplitude. In addition, the sinusoid, its amplitude and frequency will naturally serve as references for description of any alternating motion.

How then can this sinusoidal reference be used, for example, for a movement that is as little rounded as the abrupt to-and-fro between two fixed positions, which gives a 'rectangular' development with time, as already seen?

Let us examine, in a record of a period (Fig. 1.6) a sinusoid of the same frequency f, and of a suitable amplitude. The sinusoid

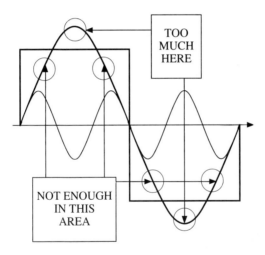

Fig. 1.6   Rectangle and sinusoid: how can one be turned into the other?

denoted by a bold line presents a good compromise. Of course, something should be added to the first and the last third of the half period, whereas, conversely, a surplus has to be taken off the second third.

But all these operations will happen quite simply, if we add to

11

the first sinusoid, a second one, of triple frequency 3*f* and again with a well-chosen amplitude (Fig. 1.6). The best choice for both amplitude and corresponding shift between one sinusoid and another is denoted by a fine line. (We cannot talk of phase difference here, because the traces recorded are not for the same frequency). The result is not illustrated, but it seems similar to the rectangle. The addition of another sinusoid, of frequency 5*f* improves things further by smoothing bumps here and there, while filling in holes. And so on. Fig. 1.7 pushes the construction as far as frequency 7*f*.

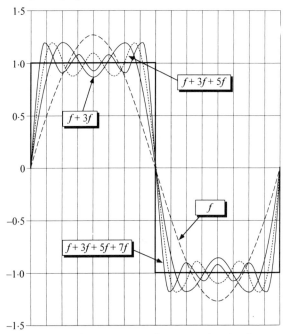

Fig. 1.7   Reconstitution of a rectangular signal

We can thank Joseph Fourier, the mathematician from Grenoble, for saving us from advancing by trial and error, when between 1768 and 1830 he gave us the few precepts that allow rapid calculation of the sinusoidal components of any period length.

All the above operations work in both directions

● if we add the right sinusoids, and thereby create the period length of any shape, the process is synthesis

● if we put filters on the complex-shaped signal and thus obtain the constituent sinusoids that make it up, it is analysis.

The sinusoid with frequency equal to that of any period length is called fundamental (or sometimes harmonic 1). Those with frequencies of $2f$, $3f$, $4f$, . . . nf, are harmonics 2, 3, 4, . . . n. Some complex but symmetrical signals contain only even or odd number harmonics.

The more harmonics a signal has the more different its trace becomes from that of a sinusoid. Many successive corrections will be needed to synthesize it correctly. Table 1.1 gives three

Table 1.1 *First harmonics of four signals with the same frequencies*

Frequency	f	$2f$	$3f$	$4f$	$5f$	$6f$	$7f$
Sinusoidal	1	0	0	0	0	0	0
Saw-tooth	0·64	0·32	0·21	0·16	0·13.	0·11	0·09
Rectangular	1·27	0	− 0·42	0	0·25	0	− 0·18
Triangular	0·81	0	− 0·09	0	0·03	0	− 0·02

examples of harmonic analysis for saw-tooth, rectangular and triangular signals, all of the same frequency f and the same amplitude A_{max}. Decay of harmonics is more rapid for the triangular signal, which is much closer to the sinusoid than the rectangular one. (The negative values indicate a change of sign between the corresponding harmonic: for example, harmonic 3 of the rectangular signal is at its maximum negative value when the fundamental is maximum positive.)

The graphic representation of the amplitude of harmonics in relation to frequency is called the spectrum. In Fig. 1.8 the first

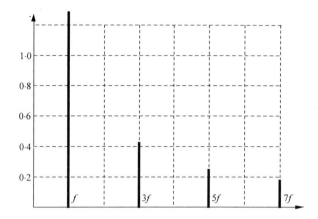

Fig. 1.8   Spectrum of a rectangular signal

harmonic components of a rectangular signal are represented. The method for breaking down the signal is spectral analysis.

Study of the behaviour (the response) of a mechanical (or electrical) structure affected by a complex-shaped oscillation often amounts to studying its behaviour for each sinusoidal component of this complex oscillation. This is the principle behind harmonic analysis of systems.

Damping

Let us go back to our mechanical mass-spring unit, but add a damping device, which produces a friction force always acting opposite to the movement. An example is a perforated piston moving inside a cylinder filled with fluid (liquid or gas).

In that case the friction force is often proportional (and opposite) to the velocity v of the displacement, which typifies viscous absorption, shown in Fig. 1.9. For a given velocity, as the velocity increases so does the force (effort) needed to overcome it. Just the displacement of the mechanical unit in air, rather than in a vacuum, is enough to create such an absorption

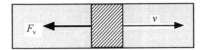

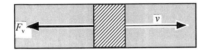

Fig. 1.9   Top to bottom: viscosity grows

(known as resistance).

In the presence of such a damper, what happens if we again move the mass away from its equilibrium position to induce oscillations? Fig. 1.10 demonstrates that this time the oscillation amplitude decreases with time. This decrease is said to be exponential. At first it is strong, because the initial amplitude—and therefore the velocity and the friction force—are high. The relative absorption diminishes along with the decrease in oscillation amplitude.

The oscillation period is also seen to increase slightly when the absorption grows. The pseudo-period is the time between two consecutive maxima, when the movement is not really periodic owing to the decrease in amplitude.

The relative damping rate is denoted by ε which varies between 0 and infinity. The first example (Fig. 1.10(a)) is for ε = 0·2.

In the second example (Fig. 1.10(b)) the viscosity of the absorption fluid has been increased (or the holes in the piston

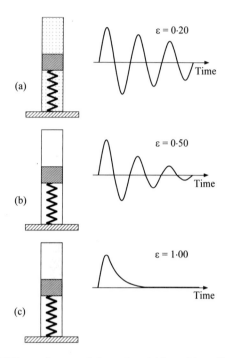

Fig. 1.10 Different degrees of absorption: (a) low; (b) medium; (c) high

give a smaller section). The damping rate $\varepsilon = 0.5$. The pseudo-period has again increased. The case where $\varepsilon = 0.707$, not shown, gives just one incursion on the other side of the rest position.

The third example (Fig. 1.10(c)) is for $\varepsilon = 1$. This time the movement is countered so much that there is no incursion to the other side of the equilibrium position. This is known as critical damping. Beyond this value, the form of the recordings remains similar, with return to equilibrium increasingly slow.

Forced oscillations and resonance

With no qualms about complicating matters, we now attach the end of the spring, originally fixed to the building, to an exciter

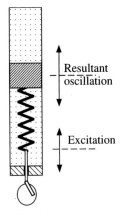

Fig. 1.11   Excitation

device, which allows it to impose a sinusoidal movement A_0 and adjustable frequency f (Fig. 1.11). We have therefore a mechanical system which would find its natural oscillation at a frequency f_n (or slightly lower with damping action), but a part of which necessarily undergoes a motion at the excitation frequency. For reasons that are difficult to explain, it is shown that after a transitory regime, lasting longer the smaller the

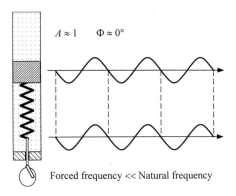

Fig. 1.12   Behaviour for low-frequency excitation

damping coefficient, the whole structure vibrates at the excitation frequency, which we therefore call forced frequency.

Figures 1.12–1.14 give the amplitudes of the mass (upper curve) and the motor (lower curve), on the same scale, for three different values of excitation frequency.

First observe what happens for a very low excitation frequency (Fig. 1.12). The movement of the mass (output) practically follows that of the exciter point (input), in both amplitude and phase. The transmission therefore equals 1. As already stated, a spring does not like changes in length: at low frequencies, the system's behaviour is dictated by the spring.

For very high values of excitation frequency (Fig. 1.13), the movement of the mass takes on a very small amplitude: 'It's too fast for me—I've hardly started in one direction when I have to change and go in the other'.

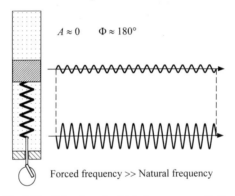

$A \approx 0 \qquad \Phi \approx 180°$

Forced frequency >> Natural frequency

Fig. 1.13 Behaviour for high-frequency excitation

Remember that a mass hates changes in velocity: at high frequencies the behaviour of the system is governed by the mass. Transmission then approaches 0 and the motions are completely opposite (180° phase difference). Somewhere between these two extreme cases, when the excitation frequency is equal to the natural frequency f_n (Fig. 1.14), a particular behaviour is obtained: the motion's amplitude can rise above

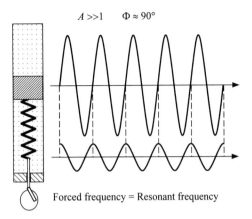

$A \gg 1 \quad \Phi \approx 90°$

Forced frequency = Resonant frequency

Fig. 1.14 Resonance

that of the motor. If this resonance is sustained, the movement of the mass is one quarter of a period out-of-phase with that of the motor. That is where the secret lies: the energy is transmitted at the right time.

The small extra force generated by the motor system is at a maximum (and each time in the right direction) at the very instant when the main force, caused by the displacement of the extremity linked to the mass, decreases to zero. Thanks to this well-timed lag, the relative magnitude of this action is enhanced—rather like the opportunities given by silences in a conversation to turn the talk towards a subject that interests you, instead of trying to do it when exchanges are at their height.

There is then an excellent coupling between the motor system and the mechanical system, and a good transfer of energy, which compensates the losses resulting from the absorption. The situation is akin to that of a child's swing with a parent 'exciter-pusher', as in Fig. 1.15, which gives us a nostalgic glance at former years.

In an ideal case, if there is no absorption, this energy-input phenomenon during each period will be expressed by continual growth in amplitude, which will become infinite.

19

Problems associated with non-absorbed resonance in built structures can be observed: physics books are full of bridge collapses caused by troops marching in step, or initiated by a gusting wind, whirling at the natural frequency of the structure.

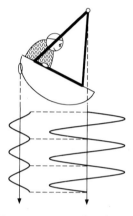

Fig. 1.15   Energy transmitted at the right moment

Figure 1.16 shows the transmission of a movement, in an equivalent undamped mass-spring system, in relation to the excitation frequency and for values of relative damping rate ε between 0·05 and 2. With the natural frequency of just the mass-spring system still f_n, a viscous fluid absorption lowers the resonance frequency f_r of (the) excited system:

$$f_r = f_n(1 - 2\varepsilon^2)^{1/2}$$

These curves reveal another aspect which will be fully exploited by the designer of noise reduction devices: if the natural frequency f_n of the system is lower than the excitation frequency f, certainly as soon as $f > 1\cdot4f_n$, a zone is reached where attenuation occurs. This is the principle behind suspended devices or viscoelastic transmission, which are dealt with in Chapter 7.

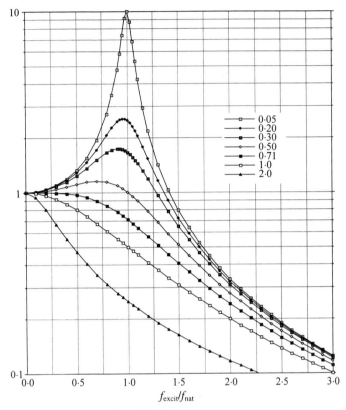

Fig. 1.16 Resonance curves

Mechanical impedance

To conclude this chapter we introduce the notion of mechanical impedance, which we will meet again later on. In an alternating movement, the system's mechanical impedance expresses the reluctance of the system to react to an excitation. As Fig. 1.3 has shown for a force that varies sinusoidally there is a corresponding sinusoidal velocity. The impedance Z is defined as the ratio of the force F to the velocity v:

$$Z = \frac{F}{v} \quad \text{or} \quad v = \frac{F}{Z}$$

v decreases when Z increases: a high impedance therefore indicates the system's refusal to take a large alternating velocity under the effect of a sinusoidal force. The choice of terminology, taken from the Latin *impedire*—hinder, resist—can easily be understood.

A system consisting simply of a mass M, subjected to sinusoidal alternating force F and frequency f, has an impedance of magnitude equal to:

$$Z_M = M(2\pi f)$$

'the more the frequency increases, the more I resist'.

For a system made up of just a spring of stiffness K, one obtains:

$$Z_K = \frac{K}{2\pi f}$$

'the more frequency increases, the less I resist'.

The expressions for the two impedances show well how there are two opposing types of behaviour in response to the frequency.

2

Propagation

Propagation of a disturbance

Figure 2.1 shows the beginning of a linear chain consisting of multiple masses and springs, attached to each other in series (the masses can be 1 mm apart for example). It is a diagrammatic, imperfect way to depict a continuous solid medium which has a certain elasticity, such as an elastic rope stretched horizontally.

Fig. 2.1   Linear chain

In the following paragraphs gravity is not considered. If kept taut, the chain at rest stays horizontal.

By attaching the left-hand end (0) of the linear chain to an agitator a motion can be induced that goes along the chain and returns to leave the chain in the at-rest position. The motion is a rapid low-amplitude vertical displacement, shown in Fig. 2.2 in relation to time. If we go over the events we will understand why

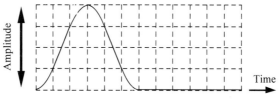

Fig. 2.2   Motion of left-hand end (0)

this motion or disturbance will propagate along the length of the structure, starting from the point of origin 0.

Figure 2.3 gives eight instantaneous snapshots, taken at 0·01 s intervals (the time-scale of Fig. 2.2) of the position of the

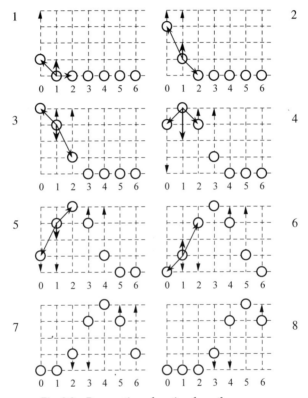

Fig. 2.3 Propagation of motion from the source

different masses neighbouring the one (furthest left) subject to movement. Arrows depict the forces exerted on one of the masses by the springs (not shown) on either side of it and also the sum of these forces. The direction of the velocity of each mass (up or down) is indicated by an arrow. The mass is in acceleration phase when the velocity and the force have the same direction, in the deceleration phase when they are opposite.

In the first shot, mass 1 is subject to a resultant upward force, whereas masses m2, m3, m4 . . . undergo forces (not depicted) that counterbalance each other. At the second instant m1 has taken up speed and is again subject to an upward force. The position of m2 is identical to that of m1 at the preceding instant. In the third frame, a braking force now acts on m1. After 0·04 s, m1 reaches its highest position. It then returns to equilibrium by the motion shown in the next four frames.

There is therefore propagation of the disturbance induced at the end of the chain. In this case the disturbance is transverse. Fig. 2.4 shows the deformation of the chain at different instants.

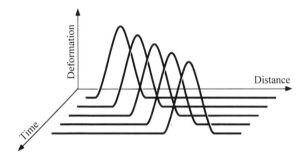

Fig. 2.4 Propagation depicted in three dimensions

In a similar way, a longitudinal disturbance could be produced, by inducing at the end a motion in the axis of the chain. It is simple to do the experiment, but not so easy to show in a diagram. The disturbance's propagation speed is called the wave speed c.

This value, the speed of propagation of the deformation, should not be confused with the speed of the different masses. Our example shows clearly that the masses' speed is directed vertically, whereas that of the disturbance is horizontal. As we might guess, the wave speed depends on the values of the quantities involved: the elementary mass, number of masses per unit length, stiffness of elementary springs, and initial tension of the chain. In our simple example, two adjacent masses describe the same movement but with a lag of 0·01 s. The velocity of disturbance propagation is therefore

$$\frac{1 \text{ mm}}{001 \text{ } s} = 01 \text{ m/s}$$

For a longitudinal disturbance, a different propagation speed will probably be found, because forces are added by a different mechanism.

When a disturbance propagates freely the value a of the displacement of a point M at instant t consequently depends on both the abscissa x of the point (its at-rest position on the axis) and the instant t considered, denoted $a(x,t)$. If there is no attenuation, each point describes the same movement as any of its neighbours, but with a time lag equal to the propagation time t_p of the disturbance over the distance d separating the two points, which with wave speed c gives

$$t_p = \frac{d}{c}$$

Each point of the propagation medium in turn acts as the source of disturbance, but with a time lag in relation to the latter.

Physics and mechanics books often start with the case of stretched vibrating strings, in which mass and elasticity are uniformly distributed. Such a vibrating string, as part of a guitar or a piano, undergoes an extremely high tension force F_T. In such conditions, the displacements from the equilibrium position are tiny and the reasoning illustrated above applies only if the modulus of F_T is taken everywhere as constant: only the direction varies. The propagation velocity then depends both on the tension and the specific mass ρ (mass per unit length, kg/m) of the string

$$c = \sqrt{\left(\frac{F_T}{\rho}\right)}$$

Propagation occurs as much in the case of planar (such as a stretched membrane, wall, water surface) or three-dimensional media (solids, liquids, gases) as in linear ones such as that just described. In planar media the deformation waves created by a source are propagated as concentric circles (Fig. 2.5), in three-dimensional media they are propagated as concentric spheres of increasing radius.

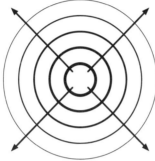

Fig. 2.5   Propagation of circular waves

Alternating and sinusoidal waves

If the excitation is maintained and if the end describes an alternating sinusoidal motion, each point in the structure will describe the same motion, with a time-lag according to the time of propagation from the source. At any given instant therefore the chain is in sinusoidal movement, as shown in Fig. 2.6.

Two points separated by a length corresponding to the distance covered by the deformation in a period of movement from the source therefore have the same motion: they are said to vibrate in phase. This distance is the wavelength λ given by

$$\lambda = cT$$

Two points separated by half a wavelength vibrate in phase opposition: one rises as the other descends.

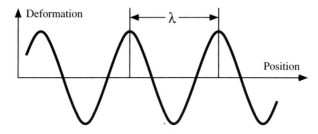

Fig. 2.6   Wavelength

As an example, the electromagnetic waves are presented in Table 2.1 classified by wavelength, period and frequency. These waves do not represent a displacement of matter but of a change in the electric and magnetic fields of the medium. They are propagated in a vacuum and in air with a speed of around 300 000 km/s. It is striking that one and the same physical phenomenon is expressed through an extremely wide range of entities (radio, light, etc.).

In solids, whether planar or three-dimensional, several types of transverse (with deformation perpendicular to the propagation) or longitudinal (deformation parallel with the propagation) deformation wave can be encountered. These waves (flexion, torsion and so on) bring into play the solids' elastic and shearing

Table 2.1   Electromagnetic waves

	Radio waves			Infrared		Visible		Ultra-Violet	X-rays		γ-rays
	LW-AM	SW-FM	μ-waves	Far	Near	Red	Violet		Soft	Hard	
f: Hz	10^5	10^8	10^{10}	10^{12}	10^{14}	5×10^{14}	10^{15}	10^{16}	3×10^{17}	10^{19}	10^{21}
λ: m	3000	3	0·03	3×10^{-4}	3×10^{-6}	$0·7 \times 10^{-6}$	$0·3 \times 10^{-6}$	3×10^{-8}	10^{-9}	3×10^{-10}	3×10^{-12}
T: s	10^{-5}	10^{-8}	10^{-10}	10^{-12}	10^{-14}	2×10^{-15}	10^{-15}	10^{-16}	3×10^{-18}	10^{-19}	10^{-21}

properties. Their propagation speed, which differs according to whether the wave is transverse or longitudinal, depends on the density of the solid, its modulus of elasticity E and its Poisson's ratio v. The order of magnitude is 500–5000 m/s.

In liquids or gases, sound waves represent the propagation of infinitesimal variations in pressure. (Sound waves do not pass through a vacuum!) Their speed in air depends on atmospheric pressure and temperature. In Table 2.2, which gives typical values, speed c is taken as 340 m/s.

Table 2.2 *Sound waves in air*

	Infrasound		Audible		Ultrasound	
			Bass	Treble	Classic	Phonons
f: Hz	0·2	20	50	5000	20 000	200×10^6
γ: m	1700	17	6·8	$6·8 \times 10^{-2}$	17×10^{-3}	$1·7 \times 10^{-6}$
T: s	5	50×10^{-3}	20×10^{-3}	$0·2 \times 10^{-3}$	50×10^{-6}	5×10^{-9}

Influence of distance from the source

Figure 2.7 shows the signal received at two points A and B situated at different distances r_A and r_B from the same source S. The horizontal interval between the two signals comes as no surprise: it results from the time of wave propagation between A and B. But why is the amplitude weaker at B ?

Let us first take the case of an isotropic source (that is to say without specific direction: it emits waves equally in all directions) and a propagation medium which is also isotropic (it allows propagation in all directions). This medium is assumed to cause no losses, in that it takes no energy from the wave.

Propagation on a plane
This example applies to circular ridges on the surface of water which has no viscosity, as in Fig. 2.5. The radiated power is distributed over the circles, whose radius r increases as the

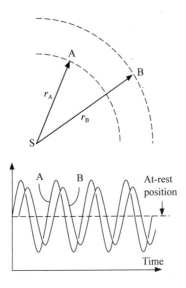

Fig. 2.7 *Effects of distance from source*

propagation continues. Therefore, for a receptor of given aperture, the power W received diminishes when r increases and the power can be expressed as inversely proportional to r

$$W = \frac{W_0 r_0}{r}$$

where W_0 is the power when the receptor is placed at r_0 from the source. (In decibels, -3dB for each doubling in radius, which will be seen in Chapter 3.)

Propagation in space
In this case the power emitted is spread over concentric spheres of increasing radius. As the surface area of a sphere is proportional to the square of its radius, the power received by a sensor of given surface area will this time be inversely proportional to the square of the distance. The fall-off is therefore more rapid than in the previous case

$$W = W_0 \left(\frac{r_0}{r}\right)^2$$

(In decibels, -6dB for each doubling of radius. See exercise 3.5.)

Linear propagation
The power emitted is in this case sustained throughout the propagation, because the dilution effect seen in the other two situations does not occur. The same result is obtained in devices using guided propagation (fibre optics, wave guides).

Absorption
To the attenuation processes resulting from power dilution with distance, is added a power loss owing to absorption by the medium, which corresponds to a change of part of the energy into heat. The decrease in useful power of the wave in the medium can then be shown to be exponential

$$W = W_0(e^{-r/L})$$

(In decibels, the fall-off is this time expressed in dB/m. See exercise 3.6.)
In the rest of this chapter, the attenuation effects will be ignored, whatever their origin.

Interference

We now assume that two identical sources of the same frequency act simultaneously and in phase. A point M (Fig. 2.8) receives simultaneously two waves, with amplitudes taken as equal, but whose effects can either be additive or subtractive depending on the distances r_1 and r_2.

Let the gap between the two distances, the step difference, $\delta = r_2 - r_1$. Depending on the position of M in relation to the two sources S1 and S2, all possible cases can be encountered between two extremes.

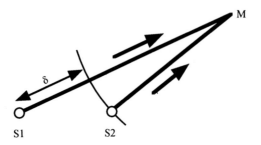

Fig. 2.8   Waves emitted from two sources, converging on M

● If δ is a whole number wavelength, the two waves arrive in phase and the resultant amplitude at M is double that which would be found with a single source

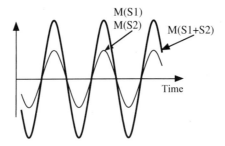

Fig. 2.9   Waves arriving in phase

(Fig. 2.9). The power received at M, proportional to the square of the amplitude, is therefore 4 times as great as that received from just one source.

● If δ is a whole number of wavelengths plus half a wavelength, the two waves arrive in phase opposition and the resultant amplitude at M is zero (Fig. 2.10). The power received by all the points obeying this condition on δ is therefore also zero.

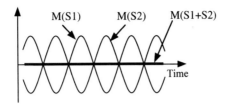

Fig. 2.10   *Waves arriving in opposition*

This turns out well for the energy balance. The total power can only be twice that of a single source and is therefore distributed between the previous points that are favoured and those that are penalized. The results given previously are inverse if the two sources S1 and S2 vibrate in phase opposition.

When δ is an intermediate value, the resultant amplitude is therefore between 0 and 2 times the amplitude in the case of a

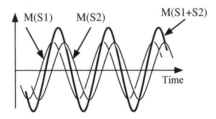

Fig. 2.11   *Combination of two waves shifted in phase*

single source (Fig. 2.11). It can be determined by calculation or graphic (Fresnel) construction with phasors (Fig. 2.12). Widely

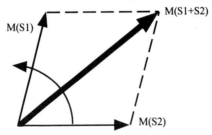

Fig. 2.12   *Method for obtaining the resultant amplitude*

used in the case of electromagnetic waves (in optics, or in old radio-navigation systems before the use of satellites, for example), this interference phenomenon will be encountered again in several forms and instances in what follows, sound waves included.

An example of the use of this phenomenon to alleviate noise is the current development of active noise-control systems. This consists of generating a counter-noise which, in a given area, weakens the received signal. Such methods are particularly judicious when the area is already equipped with loudspeakers, as in cars or passenger aircraft cabins. As will be made apparent in Chapter 3, noise strays noticeably from a pure sound with well-defined frequency and amplitude. This makes the design of active systems difficult and necessitates the use of digital signal processing. The French Building Science and Technology Centre (CSTB) employs this principle to make active windows, which give stronger insulation by controlling the pressure of the layer of air between two panes of glazing.

Directivity of a source

The interference phenomenon also explains why a source is more or less directional depending on its geometric dimensions.

Suppose that there is a source made up of a disc of diameter greater than λ where all points vibrate in phase. Each of these points can be considered as a source radiating in all directions (isotropic). What then is the overall source?

If we move away from the disc, keeping at first to its axis, all points of the source are sensibly equidistant from the receptor, placed far from the source at M. The effects are additive and the amplitude received is at a maximum.

The situation is different when the direction is at an angle θ to the axis, towards a far point M2, because the step difference δ between two points of the source is then non-negligible (Fig. 2.13). For example, for $\theta = 90°$, there will always be, for

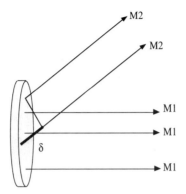

Fig. 2.13 Interferences and directivity

each point of the source, a second point such that $\delta = \lambda/2$. The energy radiated in the direction $\theta = 90°$ is therefore zero.

As a result of these interferences, there exists a direct relationship between the directivity of a source and its dimensions

- dimensions $\ll\lambda$: the source is non-directional (isotropic)
- dimensions $\gg\lambda$: the source is highly directional

The emission cone, which is the diagram of the radiation from a source, is a representation of the directivity on which is traced the amplitude received at a fixed distance R (or the square of the amplitude, corresponding to the power received), as a function of the angle of the receptor with the source axis. Fig. 2.14 gives the radiation diagram for different sources, according to the ratio between their diameter a and the wavelength. It shows how directivity increases with source diameter: from low when $a = \lambda/8$ (top left) to high when $a = 3\lambda$. When $a \gg \lambda$, other favoured directions appear, giving rise to secondary lobes, not shown here.

Five concentric semicircles on each part of Fig. 2.14 represent, by their increasing radius, the intensities received: 20, 40, 60, 80

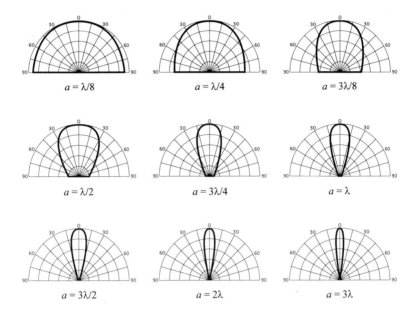

Fig. 2.14 *Source dimensions and directivity (after CSTB-REEF[1])*

and 100%. When $a = \lambda$ for example, a point at 15° from the axis receives only 75%; of the power that would be received on the axis. A source that emits several frequencies is therefore generally much more directional for the treble frequencies, for which the wavelength is smaller. A 20 cm loudspeaker will not be very directional at 100 Hz ($\lambda = 3 \cdot 4$ m), but will be highly so at 10 kHz ($\lambda = 3 \cdot 4$ cm). (A speaker system in fact comprises several loudspeakers, fitted with filters and adapted to each range of frequencies. To reduce directivity, tweeters are made small, but that is not the only reason: to equalize power, the amplitude of a low-frequency vibration is higher than that of a high-frequency one.)

A gear of a SOMFY motor, considered overall, is like a source 5 cm in diameter and 10 cm long. Directivity effects will come into play at frequencies higher than about 10 kHz.

Reflectors

It often happens that available sources are smaller than the wavelength and therefore non-directional, whereas directivity for one particular direction is needed. A reflector, with diameter greater than the wavelength λ, must then be used. The process of reflection is explained in the following section, but we can start now to consider the best choice of reflector.

Fig. 2.15 Plane reflector

We first take a plane reflector (Fig. 2.15). The source is placed in front of it and the receptor at M, far away in the direction $\theta = 0°$ and therefore almost equidistant from all points on the reflector. These points are not all reached simultaneously by a wave emitted from the source S, and so, if it is a deformation wave, they do not vibrate in phase. The waves they emit in their turn therefore arrive at M out of phase and, if the reflector is quite large, for a given point on its surface, there is always a second point such that $\delta = \lambda/2$. The resulting sum is therefore zero. The reflector therefore has no effect in the direction $\theta = 0°$: the source hides its image, given by the reflector. However, this arrangement can allow certain favoured directions θ, whose value depends on the distance between source and reflector.

We repeat the procedure with a hemispherical reflector (Fig. 2.16). In this example all the points of the latter vibrate in phase, as they are reached simultaneously by a wave coming from the source. However, they are no longer all at the same distance

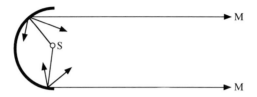

Fig. 2.16 Spherical reflector

from M, therefore there is again a step difference δ between neighbouring points and a resultant wave is obtained, due to the reflector, that is zero in the direction $\theta = 0°$.

A compromise must therefore be found between the plane surface, all of whose points are equidistant from M, but not from S, and the portion of the sphere centred on M, which has the inverse property. Was it by dint of contorting this reflector that Archimedes left us the paraboloid, a shape created by rotating a parabola around the axis passing through its focus? There is still no better way of setting up the conditions: the same distance S– M travelled, whatever the position on the reflector of the chosen

Fig. 2.17 Parabolic reflector

point, if S is at the focus and M a long distance away, at infinity in the direction of the axis (Fig. 2.17).

Snell and Descartes would have pointed out, with Fig. 2.18, and not without justification, that it is also this parabolic curve that satisfies the angle condition $i = r$ at every point on the reflector's surface and, therefore, obeys their first law.

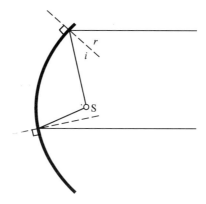

Fig. 2.18   Characteristics of the paraboloid

From waves to beams and rays

Now that, with the aid of the reflector constructed previously, we have available a perfectly directional source in the direction $\theta = 0°$, we can again consider the mechanism of rectilinear propagation of the beam so produced. In the case of a linear chain, we have noted that each point of the chain behaves in turn like a source when it starts to vibrate and carries the subsequent points with it. Exactly the same happens for a wave propagating in space. In the case of a pressure wave, every elementary volume (which is microscopic) δV reached by the wave becomes the site of pressure variations and so behaves as a source. As the volume is extremely small in relation to λ it radiates the energy as an isotropic source, as represented by an elementary cube (top of Fig. 2.19).

The question then arises: why does a parallel beam produced using the reflector travel in a straight line across air? As it continuously encounters a multitude of elementary volumes, which all radiate in all directions, shouldn't the beam quickly become completely diffused?

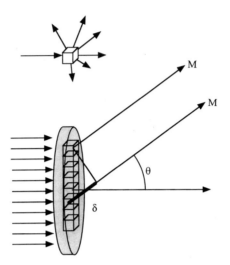

Fig. 2.19   Rectilinear propagation

Figure 2.19 shows a slice of the beam to illustrate the divergence mechanism that is expected everywhere. Once again, however, interferences occur between the radiations coming from the slice. The beam produced by the reflector inevitably has a cross-section much greater than λ. In these conditions, all the volumes of air δV located on the same straight section of the beam are reached simultaneously and radiate in phase, like an extended source. This section as a whole is in the same situation as the case we looked at previously. The radiated

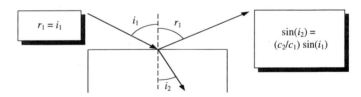

Fig. 2.20   Reflection and refraction: Snell–Descartes' laws

energy is zero in every direction—except in that of the axis. The beam's directivity is therefore self-maintaining.

This was the reasoning given by the Dutch physicist Huyghens, three centuries ago, to explain the rectilinear propagation of light, which had been found to be wave-like after the first optical interference experiments. Snell and Descartes' laws of reflection and refraction concerning the diversion of waves, as they pass from one medium of wave speed c_1 to another having a wave speed c_2, can thus be recognized and explained (Fig. 2.20).

Also explicable in this way is the diffraction of a parallel beam by an aperture smaller than or in the order of λ (Fig. 2.21). Because of the obstacle, only an elementary volume δV can be excited and, this time, there is nothing to compensate for the radiation in all directions.

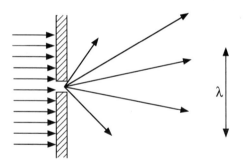

Fig. 2.21   Diffraction through a slit

This foray into the mechanisms of rectilinear propagation in a three-dimensional medium will put us on our guard, in acoustics, against representing phenomena as rays or beams as one can in geometrical optics. Rectilinear propagation of a 0·1 mm diameter laser beam with a wavelength of 0·5 μm, i.e. 200 times smaller, shows that there is little divergence. To obtain the same parallel property for a sound beam, however, at an average frequency of 1 kHz ($\lambda = 34$ cm), a beam with diameter

$200 \times 0.34 = 68$ m would be needed—and ten times the size at 100 Hz!

Geometrical representation of propagated sound really works only for extremely large rooms, although it is still sometimes convenient to use such a method.

On reflection . . .

In order to understand the mechanism proper of reflection it is worth going back to the linear chain. Now we assume that the simple disturbance, seen previously, arrives at a discontinuity in the structure: for example, quite simply, the other end of the chain, assumed to be fixed. Again, a series of snapshots (Fig. 2.22) can explain what happens. The diagrams show not only the real position of each mass, but also (shaded) the position which it would have occupied if there had been no discontinuity. The figure also shows the displacement (hatched) that should be added to that of an unimpeded point (shaded) to obtain the real position.

The last mass in the chain N is therefore fixed. From the second frame onwards we can see the disturbance suffered by the penultimate mass $N - 1$, which is subjected to a force twice as large as could have been expected. The mass $N - 1$ is therefore condemned to do a U-turn before reaching its maximum, the situation seen in the third frame, in which the high value of F can also be observed.

The fourth frame gives a misleading impression of a return to equilibrium, whereas in fact masses $N - 3$, $N - 2$ and $N - 1$ are passing to the other side, the last two at high velocity owing to the strong forces acting on them in this direction since the stage at frame two.

The process terminates in the situations of frames 5 and 6: this time the deformation is negative and propagates in the opposite direction. This effect is like that of two disturbances superimposed: a positive one which starts from the real source and moves to the right, and a negative one which comes from a

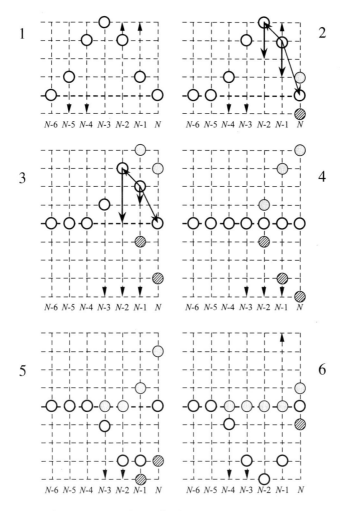

Fig. 2.22   Breakdown of reflection on a fixed point N

mirror-image source and propagates leftwards. Fig. 2.23 illustrates what happens on the other side of the imagined mirror.
   This reflection mechanism is only a generalization when there

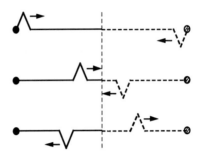

Fig. 2.23   (left) real; (right) virtual sources: fixed end at the centre

is a discontinuity in the propagation medium. This discontinuity can occur when there is a free end rather than a fixed one: it can then be shown that the reflection occurs without changing sign. The discontinuity can also result from a change in the nature of the medium, which affects the value of masses and the stiffness of springs. It is then expressed as a modification of velocity between one medium and another. In such a case, one part of the deformation continues to be propagated in the new medium, whereas the other is reflected.

In the case of a sustained alternating source, the term reflection coefficient denotes the relation between amplitudes of the reflected and incident waves. Transmission coefficient is the ratio between amplitudes of the transmitted and incident waves. The relationship between energies or powers, which are proportional to the square of the amplitude, is termed the transmission factor.

Stationary waves and modes

It may be surprising to find the term 'stationary' in a chapter devoted to wave propagation. We are going to look at two sustained waves of the same frequency but propagating in opposite directions. To simplify matters, the waves are represented by a triangular shape and, to give a starting point, they can be considered as transverse deformations which propagate.

In Fig. 2.24 the fine lines show the waves at different instants and the bold line their form when superimposed. The resultant

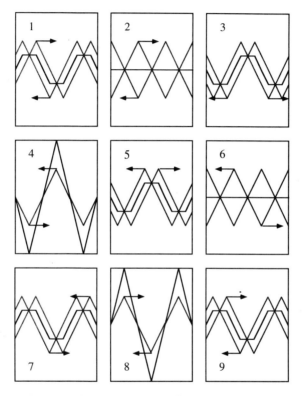

Fig. 2.24   Opposing waves: resultant stationary waves

form is expressed as a flattened triangular wave—and propagation no longer occurs. To be convinced of this refer to Fig. 2.25(a) where traces of just the nine resultants are superimposed.

Here we have a new situation. Two neighbouring points no longer have the same vertical motion, with just a time lag between them, but show a simultaneous movement, possibly in

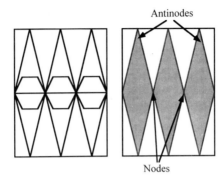

Fig. 2.25   Patterns of resultant movement

opposite directions, and have different amplitudes. Moreover, certain points do not vibrate at all (vibration nodes), whereas others do so with double amplitude (vibration antinode). The result obtained has already been seen more generally for interferences: here we are simply in the axis of the two sources S1 and S2 that produce the two waves. If images separated by much shorter time intervals are superimposed, a cone image typical of stationary waves is obtained (Fig. 2.25(b)). Two consecutive antinodes are $\lambda/2$ apart. The same applies to nodes. Exactly the same results are found with sinusoidal waves, but with a resultant which is also sinusoidal, a property which is an excellent example of the application of classic trigonometric formulae.

The remaining task is to take a big step, combining stationary waves, reflection and resonance. The starting point is again the linear chain of length L or a stretched string, now held at both ends. One of the extremities, S, is subjected to a sustained, small-amplitude vertical movement, produced by an external motor, which propagates the length of the string with wavelength λ.

Initially let $L=\lambda/2$. After sufficient time (hundredths of a second for a taut string about 1 m long) every point on the string will be subject to two waves moving in opposite directions: one from the source, the other reflected from what is really a fixed end but appears to come from a mirror-image source S′. A stationary wave is produced, with just one cone because $L = \lambda/2$. But have we in reality only two waves here?

The waves originating at S′, which propagate towards the left, will in turn be reflected at S, then propagate again to the right, as if emitted by S″, the image of S′, and so on.

The multiple reflections (as in the case of two parallel mirrors) produce an infinite number of stationary waves, which when superimposed give a resultant stationary wave of amplitude beyond comparison with that of the motor placed at S (which with hindsight justifies the consideration of S as fixed in spite of the presence of the motor).

As in any resonance phenomenon this works only if the successive waves arrive at the right time and in the right place. That occurs here because we have chosen the string length $L = \lambda/2$, which leads us to the fundamental resonance mode of the string. However, it can easily be shown that the same reasoning can be applied to several cones which correspond, for a given length of string, to a higher excitation frequency, and therefore to a smaller wavelength, by satisfying the condition

$$L = \frac{n\lambda}{2}$$

where n is an integer equal to the number of cones. Each value of n defines the mode of the string.

The vibration amplitude is therefore limited only by the energy loss resulting from absorption within the material and by the possible discrepancy in precision of the condition $L = n\lambda/2$. If, for example the excitation frequency shifts 10% away from the appropriate value, the different reflected waves superimpose with almost random phase differences, giving a very small resultant. All resonances are expressed by a high sensitivity to frequency, which is higher when the damping is weak (see Fig. 1.16). The condition $L = n\lambda/2$ shows, for a given length, which frequencies can induce a resonant system of stationary waves

$$f = \frac{nc}{(2L)}$$

For a 1 m string, and a speed of 1000 m/s, the following modes are obtained (Fig. 2.26)

1 (1 cone, $\lambda = 2\,\text{m}$) $f = 500$ Hz
2 (2 cones, $\lambda = 1\,\text{m}$) $f = 1000$ Hz
3 (3 cones, $\lambda = 067$ m) $f = 1500$ Hz
4 (4 cones, $\lambda = 050$ m) $f = 2000$ Hz.

Assume that the sinusoidal source has a frequency of 1000 Hz. It therefore stimulates the second mode of the string. But where

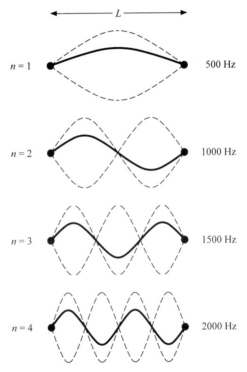

Fig. 2.26 *First four stationary modes of a stretched string*

along the string should the exciter be placed to obtain the best result?

If the exciter incites the motion at the point on the string to which it is linked, it is no good putting it at a vibration antinode, as this would condemn the antinode to have the same amplitude as the exciter. No advantage would be gained if large vibrations were needed and there would be an extremely poor coupling between the source and the resonating medium. Conversely, if the source is placed close to a vibration node, the initial configuration is again found and an antinode can be obtained that bears no comparison with that of the source. There is an excellent coupling between the source and the resonant system. In the example shown in Fig. 2.26, the source can effectively be placed at either end or even in the middle of the string, for the mode considered (mode 2).

It often happens, especially with sound and mechanical vibrations, that a source has several frequencies (various harmonics, or multiple source). For a resonating system of given geometry, several modes can be induced (for example in the case given modes 1 and 2 if the source contains the 500 and 1000 Hz frequencies simultaneously). However, the position of the source could mean that some modes are well coupled while others are much less so. If the source is put half way along the string, mode 2 will be coupled well with the source, whereas the coupling with mode 1 will be practically non-existant.

In mechanical systems where a linkage between source and construction is inevitable, if the construction has well defined modes and the source gives pure frequencies, as far as possible the points of contact will be placed at vibration antinodes so that coupling is very poor.

The possibility of inducing vibration modes exists in any two- or three-dimensional physical or mechanical system. In each case the limit conditions imposed by the geometry of the system will be satisfied for several different frequencies. In the case of a one-dimensional set-up, each mode has a characteristic whole number n. For a two-dimensional system, a plate for example, each mode has two whole numbers (m and n). The resonance frequencies of a plate of length L and width l are therefore given by

$$f_{(m,n)} = \left(\frac{c}{2}\right)\sqrt{\left(\frac{m^2}{L^2} + \frac{n^2}{l^2}\right)}$$

(Note that c is frequency-dependent for a plate).

For acoustic waves propagating inside a parallelepipedic volume with length L, width l and height h, we will have three integers (m, n, p) for each mode

$$f_{(m,n,p)} = \left(\frac{c}{2}\right)\sqrt{\left(\frac{m^2}{L^2} + \frac{n^2}{l^2} + \frac{p^2}{h^2}\right)}$$

The mode (1, 0, 0) corresponds to a system of stationary waves induced by the reflection of waves propagating only in the direction of the length L. The mode (1, 1, 1) represents a system of stationary waves induced by the reflection of waves propagating only in the direction of the diagonal of the parallelepiped, and so on. The number of modes resulting from all these combinations is infinite, but a source of given characteristics can only induce modes whose frequency is very close to its own frequencies.

The trick is therefore to know how many modes could be excited in a frequency band of given width Δf. It can be shown that, for frequencies which are high compared with the lowest resonance (that of mode 1, 0, 0), this number is

$$\frac{4\pi f^2 V \Delta f}{c^3}$$

or

$$\left(\frac{4\pi f^3 V}{c^3}\right)\left(\frac{\Delta f}{f}\right)$$

The latter form indicates that if the frequency bands are proportional, which is always the case in acoustics (with the spectrum represented by octaves or thirds of octaves, as will be seen further on), the number of modes per band is proportional to the cube of the frequency. The number of modes counted in a unit frequency band is the modal density. For example, there are 1000 times more modes to excite in the third of the octave centred on 1000 Hz (between 891 and 1122 Hz) than in that centred on 100 Hz (between 89 and 112 Hz).

In other words, once frequencies reach high levels, excitation of the very high number of modes in the structure cannot be avoided.

3

Sound as a phenomenon

What is sound?

Air has mass
A litre of air under normal conditions of temperature and pressure (22°C, 1 bar) has a mass of 1·18 g. That may not seem much, but it is enough to explain the huge value of atmospheric pressure: the force equal to the weight of air situated above a unit area.

The atmosphere extends from the ground to about 10 000 m altitude. Therefore, above a ground surface of 1 m^2, there is a volume of 10 000 m^3 (Fig. 3.1), giving a mass of 11·8 tonnes (assuming constant air density and gravity, which is far from reality); above 1 cm^2, the mass is 1·18 kg.

The real value of the mass is closer to 1 kg (density and gravity decrease with altitude), which gives a weight of about 10 N, and pressure 10 N/cm^2 ($=1$ bar $= 10^5$ N/m^2 or pascals, Pa).

Air is elastic
As we know, if air is compressed by a piston, for example when the outlet of a bicycle pump is blocked, the air exerts a return force (Fig. 3.2).

Air = masses plus springs = a favourable medium for propagation
Surrounded by air as we are, here, as in the previous chapter, we are immersed in a system of masses and springs. However, this time the system is three-dimensional. The displacement of a small volume of air brings with it a pressure change in the

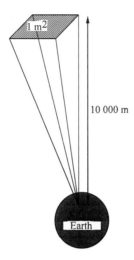

Fig. 3.1   Column of air above 1 m² surface on the ground

neighbouring volumes (Fig. 3.3), which in their turn induce other displacements, and so on. Their propagation thus finds all the necessary conditions combined and variations in pressure take place.

If it is an alternating source that creates the disturbance, there is a continuous propagation of sound waves (Fig. 3.4), expressed at every point in space by a pressure variation p_a oscillating about its equilibrium value P_0 (atmospheric pressure). The two components of sound waves in air (or in a gas) are the alternating component of atmospheric pressure and the alter-

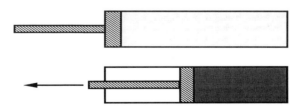

Fig. 3.2   Restoring force exerted by compressed air

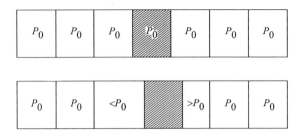

Fig. 3.3   A displacement produces pressure changes which in turn produce displacements

nating velocity of air particles, like the force and velocity in the case of mass-spring systems.

The speed of propagation of the sound waves depends on the average pressure P_0 of the air and the density ρ_0, which will depend on temperature and altitude. With temperature at 22°C and pressure at 105 Pa, the speed of the sound waves is 345 m/s.

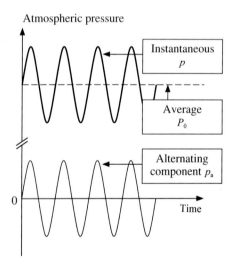

Fig. 3.4   Sound: an infinitesimal variation in atmospheric pressure

Sound sources

A sound source is therefore a device that produces alternating pressure variations.

In a rather academic way, distinction is made between sources of pressure and of displacement (Fig. 3.5). A stretched membrane, a piston or a rigid plate, stimulated by an alternating movement sets the neighbouring air particles in motion: here the source initiates an alternating variation of velocity, the same to each side of the source.

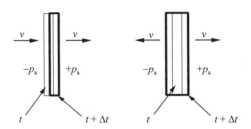

Fig. 3.5   (left) source of velocity; (right) source of pressure

Conversely, a small pulsating sphere or a pulsating wall induces, to either side of the source, pressure variations with the same sign but opposing velocities. These are referred to as pressure sources.

All that has been said regarding the influence of the geometry of a source and the close relation between dimensions, wavelength and directivity is evidently applicable to sound sources.

As will become clear further on, the threshold of perception of the human ear is equivalent to an alternating pressure variation of one ten billionth of atmospheric pressure. The amplitudes of air particle displacement corresponding to a frequency of 1000 Hz are therefore one-sixteenth of the minute distance between two atoms of a hydrogen molecule. A surface in contact with air has only to undergo very small vibrations for it to behave as a sound source, if there is a close coupling between this surface and air.

For example, the amplitude of vibrations of a 15 cm diameter loudspeaker membrane, emitting sound power of 0·2 W at 500 Hz (i.e. a level of 92 dB at 3 m), is about 30 μm. It is a hundred times greater for a frequency ten times smaller.

The human ear: structure

The human ear (and indeed that of mammals in general) is a remarkable precision instrument with highly refined structure (Fig. 3.6) and sensitivity. Its role is to convert the rapid variations in pressure p_a that constitute a sound wave into electric signals, conveyed to the brain by the auditory nerve.

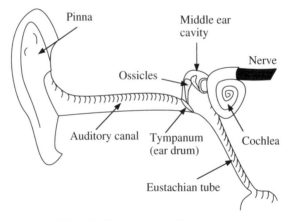

Fig. 3.6   Cross-section of human ear

The pinna acts as a funnel, increasing the receptor surface. It channels the sound waves towards the auditory canal, which terminates in a stretched membrane, the tympanum (ear drum), which can bend with the pressure differences of the sound wave. Let us examine for a moment Nature's solution to the fact that the tympanum, an extremely thin membrane, reacts to a tiny alternating sound pressure and withstands an atmospheric pressure, several million or billion times higher. This atmospheric pressure P_0 is in fact spread over the two faces of the tympanum.

The outer face of the tympanum is submitted to a pressure $P_0 + p_a$, coming from the auditory canal. Its inner face is subjected to the pressure of air from the exterior, passed through the system comprising mouth, nose, pharynx and Eustachian tube; small variations of the alternating component of the pressure are damped completely. Hence the pressure is $P_0 + p_a$ one side, P_0 on the other: only p_a acts on the tympanum and the system is a natural differential sensor (Fig. 3.7).

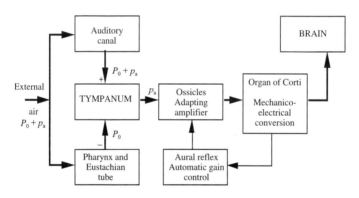

Fig. 3.7   Human hearing system

(Communication between Eustachian tube and pharynx is opened only for an instant, on swallowing. If P_0 stays constant the system functions as described above. If it changes quickly, however, owing to a drop in altitude for example, P_0 on the outer surface is no longer the same as that on the inner surface, which corresponded to the moment of swallowing. The result is a large painful deformation of the tympanum and a loss of sensitivity. The action of swallowing is sufficient to correct this.)

Attached to the middle ear, the ossicles (whose names appropriately mean hammer, anvil, stirrup) form an exceptional micro-mechanical amplifier which transmits vibrations to the inner ear. This is a tube coiled in a spiral, the cochlea, filled with a fluid that propagates the vibrations, which then act on the basilar membrane (organ of Corti) (Fig. 3.8) carrying about 15 000 ciliated cells which change the deformations which they undergo into electric signals (as do piezoelectric detectors).

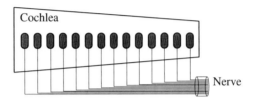

Fig. 3.8   Basilar membrane (organ of Corti)

The human ear and frequency analysis: octaves

The basilar membrane is arranged in such a way that the sound wave vibrates only certain parts, by resonance, according to the sound frequency. The brain then receives signals only from the cells concerned, which enables it to discern the sound frequency.

Even this superb device has its limitations. Signals of frequency lower than 20 Hz are generally unable to induce vibrations in this membrane and are not therefore perceived. The same goes for frequencies higher than 16 000 Hz. The audible region is in the middle of a frequency range, with infrasound at one end, ultrasound at the other. It is an average, because each individual's perception is different and there is an inevitable tendency for the passing band to shrink with age.

Another limiting factor is that we cannot usually tell the difference between a pure sound (sinusoidal, single frequency) of 2000 Hz and one at 2004 Hz with the same amplitude.

Conversely, and without having an exceptional ear, we can distinguish easily a sound of 50 Hz from another at 54 Hz, even though the absolute frequency difference is only 4 Hz.

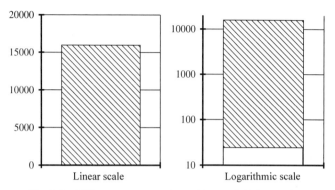

Fig. 3.9   Different representations of interval 20 Hz–16 kHz

It is not the absolute, but the relative difference that counts: the higher the frequency the lower our absolute sensitivity. The scale of frequencies is not linear, but logarithmic. If one starts at a median value, such a scale is compressed near high frequencies and dilates towards low values. Fig. 3.9 gives two representations of the interval between audible frequencies, one linear and the other logarithmic (to the base 10). On this scale, the same interval separates a frequency from another ten times as high (see the section on Logarithms at the end of this chapter).

Musicians have adopted a scale to the base 2, where the same interval separates two frequencies one of which is double the other. The interval is then called an octave.

In a chromatic scale an octave is divided into twelve semitones, all in geometric progression—in other words the frequency of a semitone is deduced from the one below it by multiplying it by a constant q ($q =$ twelfth root of 2; thus double frequency is obtained after 12 multiplications by q).

Two notes separated by an octave have the same name but a different index. A present-day piano keyboard (Fig. 3.10) goes

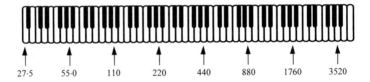

Fig. 3.10   Piano keyboard

from A_0 (27·5 Hz) to C_8 (4186 Hz) by way of 88 notes covering $7\frac{1}{3}$ octaves. The middle note, A4, occurs at 440 Hz, a common frequency for tuning forks. A sound is high-pitched (treble) when its frequency is high, low-pitched (bass) when it is low. The pitch of a sound is the image of its frequency. Furthermore, a non-sinusoidal sound necessarily contains a fundamental and harmonics. If it has few harmonics it is dull. The more harmonics it has, the more brightness it has. The same note played on two different instruments (piano and guitar for example) gives the same root frequency but different harmonics.

The human ear and sensitivity to sound intensity

For a given frequency, the ear–brain system too perceives sounds with different amplitudes of alternating pressure differently. Here again, but for different reasons, the behaviour is logarithmic, not linear. The lower the level, the higher the sensitivity; the higher the level, the lower the sensitivity (Fig. 3.11). As has already been mentioned, the system can therefore detect infinitesimal changes in pressure and react to received power of about 10^{-16} watts for an area of 1 cm^2. It still works for an intercepted power a thousand billion times greater, although the result would be unpleasant.

The human hearing system has high sensitivity and operational range (dynamics) (although in the other major receptor, the eye, these are far greater). Such qualities are not exclusive to the auditory apparatus of the human species. They stem essentially from the organ's capacity to control amplification

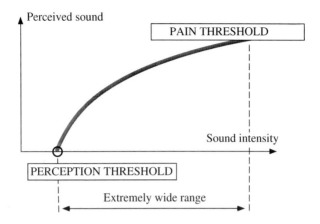

Fig. 3.11   *From perception threshold to pain threshold*

and tolerate high levels of sound while possessing a high sensitivity for low levels.

Did Nature have a predisposition for logarithms? It certainly appears so, and there are other examples. Here we see the result of evolution which, by working on the repetition of chance mutations and other influences, over millions of years, has favoured the best-adapted organs. A fierce law of natural selection ruthlessly eliminated the animal with an ear insufficiently acute to detect an approaching predator or so sensitive that it was deafened by the first clap of thunder.

In order not to exclude non-mathematical readers, a section on logarithms is included at the end of this chapter.

Power, intensity, amplitude, level: decibels

A sound source transmits energy to the surrounding air. Set in terms of time units, this energy transmitted per second represents the sound power of the source expressed in watts. This quantity (W in acoustics, which distinguishes it from pressure P) and its spectral distribution are a precise description of the source's characteristics. Except when a reflector is used, or in sealed ducting (wave guide) that channels all the power emitted, this spreads out in space. The spatial distribution, or radiation diagram, describes the directivity of the source in free space.

The sound intensity I is the power received at a point in space, per m^2 of the sensor's effective surface area, which is the surface equivalent to the sensor when oriented in the optimum direction. For example, consider a pulsating sphere of surface area 1 m^2 (radius $= 0.28$ m), emitting a sound power of 20 watts (which would be enormous). In an obstacle-free space, the spherical waves propagate. However, the energy initially held on a sphere of surface area 1 m^2 is, when 100 times further away (at 28 m), held on a sphere of $10\,000$ m^2, as the surface of a sphere is proportional to the square of its radius. The sound intensity at this distance is therefore 2 mW/m^2. A sensor with a 1 cm^2 aperture thus receives a power of 0.2 μW.

To put the intensity I of a sound in terms compatible with sound perception by human hearing, illustrated in Fig. 3.11, the logarithmic scale is used.

The sound intensity level L_I is expressed in decibels (dB) and obtained by the formula

$$L_I = 10 \, \log\left(\frac{I}{I_{\text{ref}}}\right)$$

where the logarithm is to the base 10 and has the following relations (see the section on logarithms below)

$$\log 1 = 0, \; \log 10 = 1, \; \log(A)^n = n \log(A),$$
$$\log(AB) = \log(A) + \log(B)$$

and if $X = \log(x)$ then $x = 10^{(x)}$

The value $L_I = 0$ dB corresponds to $I = I_{\text{ref}}$. The reference intensity $I_{\text{ref}} = 10^{-12}$ W/m^2 has been adopted, which is the value of the average threshold of perception.

Similarly, because any increase in power leads to a proportional increase in intensity, the sound power level L_W of a source is also expressed in decibels, and determined by the same formula

$$L_W = 10 \, \log\left(\frac{W}{W_{ref}}\right)$$

The value $L_W = 0$ dB corresponds to $W = W_{ref}$. The reference taken as W_{ref} is 10^{-12} watt.

Sensors often do not give a direct measure of power, but measure a physical quantity whose square gives the energy or the power. For example, in the case of sound waves, the sensor used will be one for pressure or acceleration, from which the velocity is deduced. The sound intensity at a point is proportional to the square of the effective value of the alternating component P of the pressure at that point (see Appendix 1)

$$I = kP^2 = \left(\frac{1}{\rho_0 c}\right)P^2 = \frac{1}{(400)}P^2 \quad \text{(in air)}$$

Representation as levels incorporates the desire that one value in decibels represents both the sound intensity and the amplitude of the parameter (pressure, velocity) associated with it. There are two consequences of this

- use of the fact that if I is proportional to P^2, then $\log I$ is proportional to $\log P^2 = 2 \log P$
- natural choice of equivalent reference levels for I_{ref} and P_{ref}^2, then $I_{ref} = (1/400) \, P_{ref}^2$

The sound pressure level L_P, in decibels, can therefore be defined

$$L_P = 20 \, \log\left(\frac{P}{P_{ref}}\right)$$

The value $L_P = 0$ dB corresponds to $P = P_{ref}$. For reference $P_{ref} = 2 \times 10^{-5}$ Pascal has been taken as it is the average threshold of perception. In contrast, atmospheric pressure is 1015 hPa, almost ten billion times as great.

Comparison and addition of levels

It takes a little practice to become familiarized with the levels expressed in decibels. To this effect several examples are brought together to illustrate different situations that will be encountered further on.

Exercise 3.1: convergence of power into decibels
'What is the sound power level of the 40 watt hi-fi system my son wants for his birthday?'

The figure on the equipment label is in fact the electrical power transmitted to the speakers and not the converted sound power which is far lower. Nevertheless, we will here assume that this power would be fully converted into sound power (Fig. 3.12)

$$L_W = 10 \log \left(\frac{W}{W_{ref}} \right) = 10 \log \left(\frac{40}{10^{-12}} \right) = 136 \text{ dB}$$

Fig. 3.12   2 × 20 watts = 136 dB

This is the power level achieved by a private plane. Under pressure from the neighbours, the volume dial will be kept sensibly low.

Exercise 3.2: conversion of decibels into power
'A murmured conversation has an average level L_W of 30 dB. What is the corresponding sound power?'

$$W = W_{ref} \, 10^{0.1 L_W} = 10^{-12} \times 10^3 = 10^{-9} \text{ watt}$$

Exercise 3.3: addition of two equal powers
'I simultaneously use two sources of the same power W. What is the total $L_{W'}$ corresponding to the power $W' = 2W$?'

$$L_W = 10 \, \log\left(\frac{W}{W_{ref}}\right)$$

$$L_{W'} = 10 \, \log\left(\frac{W'}{W_{ref}}\right) = 10 \, \log\left(\frac{2W}{W_{ref}}\right)$$

$$= 10 \, \log\left(\frac{W}{W_{ref}}\right) + 10 \, \log(2) = L_W + 3 \text{ dB}$$

The logarithm of a product AB is equal to the sum of the logarithms of A and B.

If the power of the source is doubled, 3 dB is added to the initial power level.

Checking for $W = 40$ watts

$$L_W = 10 \, \log\left(\frac{W}{W_{ref}}\right) = 10 \, \log\left(\frac{40}{10^{-12}}\right) = 136 \text{ dB}$$

$$L_{W'} = 10 \, \log\left(\frac{W'}{W_{ref}}\right) = 10 \, \log\left(\frac{80}{10^{-12}}\right) = 139 \text{ dB}$$

There is indeed a difference of 3 dB.

If power is multiplied by 10, 10 dB must be added.

Exercise 3.4: addition of different powers
'Consider two sources, one with level L_{W_1} of 54 dB, the other with $L_{W_2} = 41$ dB. We can detect a catch concerning the total level: surely it is not 95 dB?'

Indeed it is not. It has just been noted that if two sources each give 54 dB, like the more powerful source in the question, the overall level would always be only $54 + 3 = 57$ dB.

What are the values for the corresponding powers? Using the procedure in exercise 3.2, the calculation is

$$10^{-12} \times 10^{(0.1 \times 5.4)} = 251\ 10^{-9}\ \text{watt}$$
$$10^{-12} \times 10^{(0.1 \times 4.1)} = 12.6\ 10^{-9}\ \text{watt}$$
$$L_W = 10\ \log\left(\frac{W}{W_{\text{ref}}}\right) = 10\ \log\left(\frac{264\ 10^{-9}}{10^{-12}}\right) = 54.2\ \text{dB}$$

In other words, the total level is practically equal to that of the most powerful source, since the gap between them is so large: one is 20 times as powerful as the other.

Let us find this ratio of powers without performing the effective calculation for them

Difference of 13 dB between L_{W_1} and $L_{W_2} = 10\ \text{dB} + 3\ \text{dB}$
= multiplication by 10 + multiplication by 2
= multiplication by 20.

Figure 3.13 gives another example.

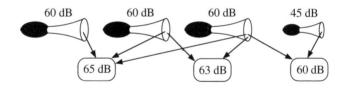

60 dB   60 dB   60 dB   45 dB

65 dB   63 dB   60 dB

Fig. 3.13   Addition of powers expressed as levels

Practical rules for busy acoustics engineers (after SRL[2])

If difference between levels to be added is	The total is the higher level plus
0 or 1 dB	3 dB
2 or 3	2
4 to 9	1
greater than 10	0

Exercise 3.5: weakening with distance
'How does the intensity level L_I intercepted by a receiver decrease when it is moved away from a source emitting spherical waves?'

In a non-absorbing medium, the energy on a sphere stays constant when its radius R increases. For two successive radii R_1 and R_2

$$I_2 = \frac{W_2}{S_2} \quad I_1 = \frac{W_1}{S_1} \quad W_1 = W_2 \quad S_1 = 4\pi R_1^2 \quad S_2 = 4\pi R_2^2$$

Therefore

$$\frac{I_2}{I_1} = \frac{S_1}{S_2} = \left(\frac{R_1}{R_2}\right)^2 = \frac{I_2 I_{ref}}{I_1 I_{ref}}$$

$$10 \log\left(\frac{I_2 I_{ref}}{I_1 I_{ref}}\right) = 10 \log\left(\frac{R_1}{R_2}\right)^2 = 20 \log\left(\frac{R_1}{R_2}\right)$$

$$10 \log\left(\frac{I_2}{I_{ref}}\right) - 10 \log\left(\frac{I_1}{I_{ref}}\right) = 20 \log\left(\frac{R_1}{R_2}\right)$$

$$L_{I_2} - L_{I_1} = -20 \log\left(\frac{R_2}{R_1}\right)$$

If $R_2 = 10\, R_1$, then $L_{I_2} - L_{I_1} = -20$ dB therefore
  Attenuation $= -20$ dB/ten times multiplication of distance
If $R_2 = 2\, R_1$, then $L_{I_2} - L_{I_1} = -6$ dB therefore
  Attenuation $= -6$ dB/doubling of distance

Exercise 3.6: attenuation of a guided wave in an absorbent medium
'If the wave is channelled, unlike in the previous case the attenuation does not occur by energy distribution in an increasingly large space, since the wave is guided, but by dissipation in the material inside the guide. How then is the weakening of the wave expressed?'

The volume which the wave crosses is divided into elementary slices of thickness dr. The power lost dW (a negative value) in each slice is proportional to

- an attenuation coefficient k
- the power W crossing the slice
- the thickness dr of the slice.

$$dW = -kW dr$$

The size of k is the inverse of a length and depends on the material. Once integrated (see Logarithms below), the differential equation gives

$$W = W_0 e^{-kr}$$

In an absorbing medium there is a consequent exponential decrease of the power transmitted. In terms of levels we have

$$L_W = L_{W_0} - (10/2 \cdot 3)kr$$

The attenuation in dB is therefore directly proportional to the distance r travelled by the wave in the medium and is expressed as dB/m or dB/km. For example

- a sound beam at 1000 Hz in air at 20°C and 30% relative humidity: 0·005 dB/m. This is a very weak attenuation. A well guided sound wave in air does not lose power quickly (as with a loudhailer)
- a light wave in a high-quality silica optic fibre: 0·15 dB/km. (A repeater amplifier every 500 km is sufficient if it supplies a boost of +75 dB.)

Exercise 3.7: effects of plane reflectors
'As a general rule, a source is never isolated in space, but positioned near at least one reflector, the wall to which it is attached or the floor. A sound intensity I' results, higher than I obtained with the source on its own, by addition of the direct and reflected beams. The directivity factor Q is the multiplication coefficient for the difference between I and I'. In terms of levels, $L_{I'} > L_I$.

If all interference effects are ignored, what must be added to L_I to obtain $L_{I'}$ if one of the following is placed behind the source

(a) a plane reflector
(b) two plane reflectors at 90° (forming a dihedron)
(c) three plane reflectors at 90° (forming a trihedron)?

In case (a), in the half of the space containing the source, the power received is doubled ($Q=2$), which amounts to the addition everywhere of 3 dB, therefore

$$I' = 2I \quad L_{I'} = L_I + 3 \text{ dB}$$

In (b), in the quarter of the space containing the source, four times the amount of power is received ($Q=4$)

$$I' = 4I \quad L_{I'} = L_I + 6 \text{ dB}$$

In (c), the power emitted by the source is distributed over one-eighth of the space. The resulting level is 8 times as high ($Q=8$) in this favoured zone containing the source

$$I' = 8I \quad L_{I'} = L_I + 9 \text{ dB}$$

Exercise 3.8: third-octave wavebands
'When one goes from one one-third octave band to the next, what is the multiplication of the frequencies? What are the upper and lower limits of the one-third octave band centred on 100 Hz?'

If a one-third octave band is run through from one end to the other, the starting frequency is multiplied by a number q, such that a multiplication factor of 2 is obtained, if the process is repeated three times, since the frequencies at the two ends of an octave are in a ratio of 2

$$q = \sqrt[3]{2} = 1\cdot 26$$

The same reasoning applies if this band is split into two: going through the whole of a one-sixth octave band, the initial frequency is multiplied by a number q', to obtain a multi-plication factor of 1·26 if the operation is repeated twice, because the frequencies at either end of a one-third octave band are in a ratio 1·26

$$q' = \sqrt{1\cdot 26} = \sqrt[6]{2} = 1\cdot 12$$

The one-third octave band centred on 100 Hz is therefore situated between frequencies

$$\frac{100}{1\cdot12} = 89\,\text{Hz} \quad \text{and} \quad 100 \times 1\cdot12 = 112\,\text{Hz}$$

Physiological correction

There are enough advantages in decibel scales for us to adopt this system, which provides the user with a tool of uncommon finesse and subtlety, as will be seen in the descriptions of attenuation. What has just been covered regarding the addition of sound powers of different sources must now be linked to the ear's frequency sensitivity. A source with a given sound power does not have the same effect at frequencies of 10 Hz or 1000 Hz or 100 Hz. This is the case within the audible domain itself. For

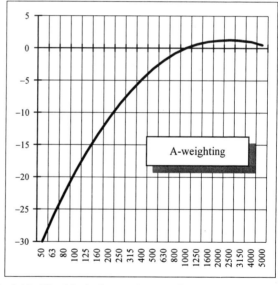

Frequency (Hz)	Correction (dB)
50	−30
63	−26
80	−22·5
100	−19·1
125	−16·1
160	−13·4
200	−10·9
250	−8·6
315	−6·6
400	−4·8
500	−3·2
630	−1·9
800	−0·8
1000	0
1250	0·6
1600	1
2000	1·2
2500	1·3
3150	1·2
4000	1
5000	0·5

Fig. 3.14 Physiological correction type A

the same power, low-frequency sources have a weaker effect than those emitting frequencies in the range where sensitivity is most acute: between 1 and 5 kHz.

For each frequency, the power is therefore multiplied by a coefficient, or a correcting figure is added to the level expressed in decibels. Several types of correction are possible. The one most used, correction A, is shown in Fig. 3.14 with its values for different frequencies and the corresponding curve. In each one-third octave band, the correction is applied to the individual power or pressure levels by adding the value indicated. The overall weighted level is obtained by logarithmic summation of the individual levels. To avoid ambiguity, the pressure, intensity and power of the sound thus corrected are called weighted sound pressure, weighted sound intensity and weighted sound power. The method of weighting used for these corrected levels is indicated by A, B or C. We will speak for instance of a 30 decibel A-weighted sound pressure level: 30 dB(A). Unweighted values are expressed in dB(lin).

Table 3.1   Sound power levels L_W

Power: watts	L_W: dB(A)	Source
100 000	170	Jet aircraft
10 000	160	—
1000	150	—
100	140	—
10	130	Private plane
1	120	1 MW turbogenerator
0·1	110	Pneumatic drill
0·01	100	Car at 130 km/h
0·001	90	Portable leaf
0·0001	80	blower
0·000 01	70	Standard clothes dryer
0·000 001	60	Standard washing machine
0·000 000 1	50	Super-quiet washing machine
0·000 000 01	40	Worker sweeping leaves
0·000 000 001	30	Human voice: light murmur

Typical values of sound levels L_W and L_P

Typical values of A-weighted sound power and pressure levels are shown in Tables 3.1 and 3.2 as a reference for orders of magnitude. The power level is largely used to describe the amount of sound made by motorized equipment, whereas the pressure level or the intensity level makes sense only at a given point (distance from the source is always given, except when the sources are diffuse or situated in a reverberation room where the level is uniform).

Table 3.2 Sound pressure levels L_P

L_P: dB(A)	Source
130	36 kW siren 30 m away
120	Inside a boilerworks
110	Jet aircraft on take-off (at 100 m) Maximum level for 'walkman' radios sold in France
100	Pneumatic drill, position of user
90	Danger level for 8 h of exposure Average listening level for 'walkman' radios in France
80	Motorway or goods train at 30 m Maximum level for 'walkman' radios sold in Japan
70	Limit of intelligibility of person talking close by Vacuum cleaner 3 m away Heavy city traffic (at building façade)
60	Light urban traffic, measured at façade
50	Quiet restaurant
40	Quiet urban residential area at night
30	Country area far from roads
20	Inside a record studio room
10	Silence
0	Threshold of perception (young people, 1000–4000 Hz)

Logarithms

For the reader who is unfamiliar with such mathematical entities, we will justify the treacherous presence of exponential functions and logarithms that appear in many physical, statistical and natural laws. These functions represent events which have a value y whose variation rate in relation to the variable x (on which y depends) obeys a simple relation of proportionality, either with y itself or with the inverse of x.

Variation rate
In order to define the notation, recall that the variation rate of a quantity y as a function of variable x on which it depends simply expresses the ratio of the variation of y to that of x when these variations become weak enough for the curve $y(x)$ to approximate a straight line (Fig. 3.15).

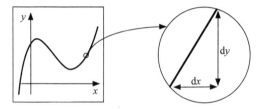

Fig. 3.15 *Variation rate*

These variations are therefore denoted dy and dx and the rate of variation is written: dy/dx.

Exponential law
In a phenomenon that obeys an exponential law, the variation rate is proportional to y

$$\frac{dy}{dx} = ky$$

This law represents behaviour of the type

'*The more there is already, the more it will increase further*'.

Each individual can associate y with any familiar quantity: stacks of files on a desk, invested capital, fiscal pressure, number of nuclear fissions in a non-controlled chain reaction, pairs of rabbits.

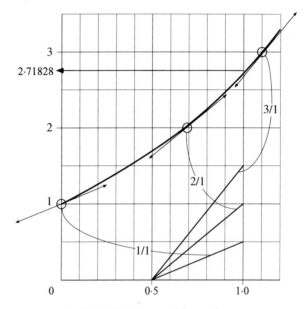

Fig. 3.16   Exponential growth

A starting value for y is, of course, needed in order to trace the progress of such behaviour. An initial y of 0 will give rise to zero growth rate and therefore a stationary value of y. A starting value of $y = 1$ is more interesting : it gives a growth rate of 1 if k is also 1. It is a neutral, balanced choice which is highly convenient as a start: anything can happen! This will therefore be used to follow the subsequent path of y (Fig. 3.16). As y increases, so its growth rate increases further. When y reaches 2, it grows twice as quickly as x, and when it reaches 3, three times as rapidly, and so on. This growth is progressive, but extremely rapid. If no factor intervenes to counterbalance such exponential effects, it will reach explosion level.

The relation between y and x is written: $y = e^x$. This gives $e^0 = 1$ and $e^1 = 2.718 = e$.

Logarithmic law

In a phenomenon that obeys a logarithmic law, the variation rate is inversely proportional to the variable x: $dy/dx = k'/x$. This law is an expression of behaviours of the type

> *'The stronger the driving phenomenon, the smaller the effect it has'.*

Once again this could cover a wide range of events. We have just seen in this chapter the extent to which the ear obeys the self-saturation principle. This is also apparent in electrical circuits (in capacitors for instance).

In the case where k' is removed by making it 1, one can start with $x = 1$, as previously with an equilibrated growth rate. What happens next? See Fig. 3.17.

The rate of increase does not cease to diminish: 1/1 for $x = 1$, 1/2 when $x = 2$, then 1/3 for $x = 3$. Growth continues, certainly, but more and more slowly. The relation between y and x is: $y = ln(x)$. Therefore $ln(1) = 0$ and $ln(2.718) = ln(e) = 1$.

These logarithms, with symbol ln, are called Napierian, after the Scottish mathematician Napier who brought them into being in 1614.

In Figs 3.16 and 3.17 the logarithmic law is shown to be the reciprocal of the exponential law: one passes from one to the other by swapping x and y

$$\frac{dy}{dx} = y \leftrightarrow \frac{dx}{dy} = x \quad \text{or} \quad \frac{dy}{dx} = \frac{1}{x}$$
$$y = ln(x) \leftrightarrow x = e^y$$
$$x = ln(y) \leftrightarrow y = e^x$$

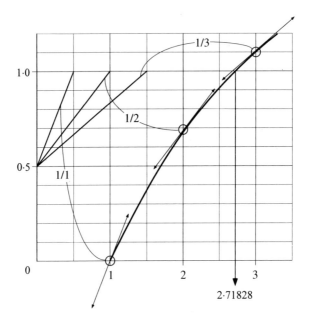

Fig. 3.17 Construction of a logarithmic curve

Decimal logarithm

We have simplified matters by adopting a coefficient k' of 1, which gives a unitary growth rate when $x = 1$. At this point, a smaller growth rate could be chosen, which amounts to taking another value of k', also smaller. Considering our usual arithmetical habits, based on our set of ten fingers, an interesting choice consists in taking an initial growth rate such that x has to reach 10 before y becomes 1. This option leads to decimal logarithms, or 'logs'. It is expressed by the curve on Fig. 3.18, with an initial growth rate of 0.435, therefore smaller by a factor of 2.3 than the unitary rate of a Napierian logarithm.

When x reaches 10, the growth rate of y is by definition one-tenth of its value (0.435/10) when $x = 1$. If this point $x = 10$ is taken as the new starting point, we therefore need 10 times as

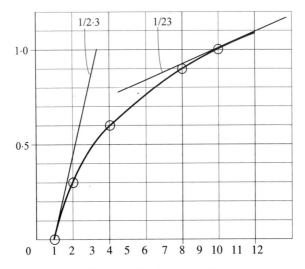

Fig. 3.18   Decimal logarithms

much variation on x to move y from 1 to 2 than was required to go from 1 to 0. It is therefore when x reaches 100 that y equals 2. The growth rate is then 1/100 of its starting value, and by the same token x must this time reach 1000 before y is 3.

With decimal logarithms

$$y = \log(x) \leftrightarrow x = 10^{(y)}$$
$$x = \log(y) \leftrightarrow y = 10^{(x)}$$

Logarithm of a product
In the notation dx and dy introduced to express the variation rate dy/dx, d simply means 'any small variation of . . .' and infinitely small at that. Thus dy represents a tiny variation of y, small enough to fit the curve $y(x)$ to a straight portion of a straight line.

By the general definition of logarithms ('log')

$$\frac{dy}{dx} = \frac{k'}{x} \quad \text{or} \quad dy = d(\log(x)) = k' \, \frac{dx}{x}$$

If we now take a product S of two quantities a and b, which will increase by da and db, what is the increase dS of the product ab? The initial value is $S = ab$. The new value will be

$$S + dS = (a + da)(b + db) = ab + bda + adb + dadb \quad \text{or}$$
$$dS = bda + adb + dadb = bda + adb$$

where da and db are assumed to be infinitely small compared with a and b. The term $dadb$ is therefore negligible in relation to the others, which are themselves minute, which explains why they disappear.

Dividing now by $S = ab$ gives

$$\frac{dS}{S} = \left(\frac{da}{a}\right) + \left(\frac{db}{b}\right)$$

(Note in passing the use that can be made of such an equation to calculate the relative variation of a product when the relative changes in each of the terms are known, provided that the variations are small: if one of the terms changes by $+0.5\%$ and the other changes by -0.3%, their product will change by $+0.2\%$.) To link the latter expression to the definition of logarithms, it is sufficient to multiply everything by k', to obtain

$$d(\log S) = d(\log a) + d(\log b)$$

Now, the sum of the variations is equal to the variation of the sum

$$d(\log S) = d(\log a + \log b)$$

Moreover, two quantities that change by the same amount themselves differ by only a constant C. This results in

$$\log S = \log(ab) = \log a + \log b + C$$

Assume $b = 1$. As log 1 is 0, C must be 0, therefore

$$\log(ab) = \log a + \log b$$

and in particular

$$\log a^n = n \log a$$

4

Sound propagation and attenuation in rooms

Attenuation and distance

The best way to protect oneself from the effects of a sound source is, naturally, to move away from it. This precept can only be completely tested in ideal, free field conditions, i.e. without the slightest obstacle to wave propagation. If there is a point source or, which amounts to the same thing, if the source is non-directional and far enough away from the receptor, the sound waves are spherical. The disturbance reaches all points at an equal distance d from the source simultaneously, causing them to vibrate in phase. The further away from the source, the more points are reached by the disturbance. Their number increases like the surface area of a sphere, and therefore like the square of the distance from the source (see Exercise 3.5 and Appendix 1).

The vibration energy, transmitted at every instant by the source, set in terms of unit time, corresponds to the sound power. This power becomes distributed over an ever-growing number of points as distance from the source increases. The sound intensity captured by a given receptor therefore diminishes as the square of the distance from source increases: it is reduced to one-quarter if d is doubled, to one ninth if this is tripled.

Expressed as an intensity level this law is written

L_I decreases by 6 dB for each doubling of distance from the source.

For a freely propagating wave, the intensity is proportional to the square of the amplitude of the alternating component of the pressure. The latter therefore decreases proportionally with distance. However, because in the expression for levels the appropriate multiplication factor is 20 rather than 10, the same can be said for pressure level (Fig. 4.1).

L_P decreases by 6 dB for each doubling of distance from the source.

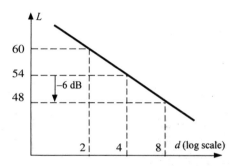

Fig. 4.1   Fall-off of levels with distance

Reverberation

In practice, free field conditions are rare unless extreme precautions are taken. Even out of doors there are ground reflections that must be taken into account. Reflections considerably reduce the attenuation caused by distance and can even cancel it out.

To check that this is really the case, consider the effects of a parabolic reflector, with the source at its focus. Under ideal conditions the reflector does not perceive any attenuation as long as it is in the reflected beam, however distant. Outside the path of this beam, however, there is complete attenuation.

In an enclosed room, sound wave reflection from all the walls is called reverberation. This effect explains why the voice carries much further in a room than outside and it is the basis of studies in interior acoustics. If the walls are perfect reflectors, the sound energy will be reflected many times and will spread evenly through the entire volume, as if there were many virtual sound sources and possible images owing to the multiple reflections from the mirrors formed by the walls (Fig. 4.2). This is the case of a reverberated or diffuse field.

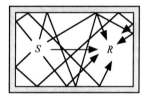

Fig. 4.2   Multiple reverberation on walls

In a room with ideal reverberation conditions, the level measured in the space should grow indefinitely in the presence of a continued sound source (a permanent supply of energy) and should be preserved indefinitely even after the source is switched off, like a perpetual echo. In practice, the walls naturally cannot be perfect reflectors. They transmit some of the vibrations to the exterior or absorb them, or both. The acoustic energy therefore cannot grow indefinitely in the presence of a source because part of it is dissipated in the walls.

The limiting case is where the walls are completely absorbent, which brings us back to free field conditions. It is exploited in anechoic rooms. In the intermediate case of partial reflection, true for almost all situations, the two types combine: free field close to the source and reverberated field away from it; reflection effects take on a great significance. A space with highly absorbent wallcoverings but normal floor is semi-anechoic (or hemi-anechoic: the walls mainly absorb energy whereas the hard floor reflects it). Fig. 4.3 illustrates the three situations: ideal anechoic room, ideal reverberation room and usual case. Regarding intermediate situations, we speak of a live room when the amount of sound reflection is relatively small (but not so small as in a perfect reverberation room) and we will call it a dead room if the amount of absorption is quite large (but not so much as in a perfect anechoic room).

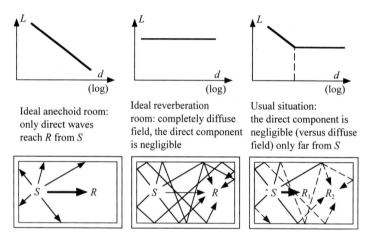

Fig. 4.3   *Fall-off of levels with distance in three situations*

Because the walls absorb or transmit part of the energy, switching off the source, in a real situation, causes a reduction in the sound energy stored in the volume. It can be shown (see Appendix 2) that this decrease is exponential: for example 90% of the energy W disappears in unit time t, which leaves $W/10$ after t, $W/100$ after $2t$, $W/1000$ after $3t$ and so on.

In terms of levels on the logarithmic scale this decrease is linear. The time taken for the level to fall by 60 dB (initial intensity divided by 1 million) defines the reverberation time T_R of the room (Fig. 4.4).

In an ideal anechoic room, T_R is zero (a value below 0.1 s in

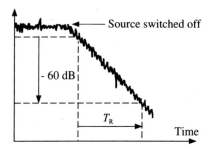

Fig. 4.4 Reverberation times

practice). In an ideal reverberation room, T_R is infinite (greater than 5 s in practice). A furnished living room for example has a T_R of around 0·5 s. A conference room must be slightly reverberating, so that a speaker does not have to raise his voice, but not too much or successive syllables will overlap and necessitate a slow, articulated delivery. A cathedral will have a T_R of about 5–10 s.

Absorption

Absorption by dissipation

Sound absorption by dissipation is a transformation mechanism, of vibration energy into thermal energy. For absorption to occur, the contact surface between air and material must be as large as possible for a given volume: a situation met in porous materials. Extensive rubbing together of air particles and the material leads to heat dissipation and a reduction in vibration energy.

Absorption can also result from movement induced in particles of the material itself and dissipation by friction at the core of the material. In most cases absorption by dissipation increases with the frequency of the sound wave.

Sound-absorbent materials can be fibrous (fibreglass, rock wool, plaster/fibres compounds, wood fibre) or cellular of open-cell type (clay foam, cellular concrete, flexible foam polyurethane, foam, asbestos, cork). Materials with closed cells (expanded polystyrene, stiff foam polyurethane) are good thermal insulators but poor acoustic absorbers. Plaster without a coat of rendering is one of the most economical absorbing materials.

Absorbant materials are used much more in wall coverings to reduce reflections from a wall or partition, than to influence its transmission properties. This explains why the absorption coefficient α, which is characteristic for the different materials, corresponds to a reflection test, where the material is put on to a reflecting wall surface.

The value α expresses the proportion of vibration energy which, arriving from all directions on to the material, is not reflected. If $\alpha = 0$, there is zero absorption and total reflection. If $\alpha = 1$, there is total absorption but no reflection.

The absorption coefficient depends on the thickness, and assemblage of the material (Table 4.1). When the reflection

Table 4.1 Absorption coefficient of different materials

Frequency: Hz	125	250	500	1000	2000	5000
Glass: 3 or 4 mm	0·20	0·15	0·10	0·07	0·05	0·05
Glass thickness > 4 mm	0·10	0·07	0·04	0·03	0·02	0·02
Concrete, granular cement	0·02	0·02	0·02	0·04	0·05	0·05
Plaster spread on heavy wall	0·03	0·03	0·02	0·03	0·04	0·05
Acoustic plaster, spread	0·30	0·35	0·50	0·70	0·70	0·70
Separated plaster panel	0·30	0·15	0·10	0·05	0·40	0·05
Perforated metal + absorbent	0·20	0·55	0·80	0·80	0·80	0·75
Carpeting/flock wall covering	0·10	0·15	0·25	0·30	0·30	0·30
Thick curtain	0·05	0·15	0·35	0·55	0·65	0·65
Mineral wool 25–50 mm	0·15	0·35	0·65	0·80	0·75	0·70

coefficients $\alpha_1, \alpha_2 \ldots \alpha_n$, of materials covering surfaces $S_1, S_2, \ldots S_n$, of a room of volume $V(m^3)$ are known, the room's reverberation time T_R (s) can be predetermined, by using Sabine's formula (see Appendix 2)

$$T_R = \frac{0 \cdot 16V}{A}$$

In this formula A (m^2) is the equivalent absorption area (or Sabine absorption)

$$A = \alpha S \text{ or } A = \alpha_1 S_1 + \alpha_2 S_2 + \ldots + \alpha_n S_n$$

in other words an overall surface, weighting each surface of the room by its coefficient of absorption. The reverberation time becomes greater the smaller the absorbing surface area.

Absorption by resonating technique
The absorption technique consists of creating resonance of an element placed against the wall where reflection has to be minimized. At the resonance frequency the energy transfer between the incident wave and the resonating device is at a maximum, therefore the reflected wave is weakened.

The simplest device of this type is the plane resonator, or reflector panel. It consists of a solid panel (wood, plasterboard, sheet metal), separated from the wall by a layer of air, with or without an absorbing material (Fig. 4.5). The resonance frequency f depends on the surface mass m of the material (kg/m^2) and thickness d (m) of the air layer

$$f = \frac{60}{\sqrt{(md)}}$$

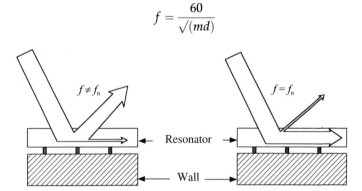

Fig. 4.5   Effect of inducing resonance in a panel

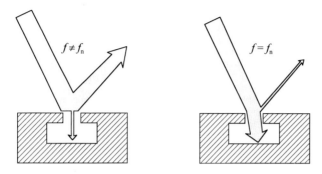

Fig. 4.6   Effect of inducing resonance in a cavity

Another kind of resonator currently used incorporates a network of Helmholtz cavities: each cavity is linked to the external medium by a duct (of length *l*, aperture *S*) and acts as a resonator, whose absorption frequency depends on the geometry (Fig. 4.6). Consequently this frequency is higher the smaller the dimensions of duct and cavities. This effect explains the sound absorption properties of perforated bricks, or of concrete blocks open to the exterior. It is common to use a metal panel or perforated wood, as shown in Fig. 4.7, which explains why one

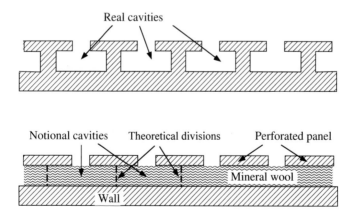

Fig. 4.7   Perforated panel: principle and practical construction

can do without physical separation between cavities without jeopardizing the final results. This simplification allows for ease of manufacture. An absorbent material is usually inserted between the perforated sheet and the wall or partition. Helmholtz resonators are much more efficient than other absorption mechanisms, but in a much narrower frequency range (Fig. 4.8).

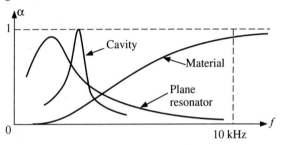

Fig. 4.8   Absorption achieved by different techniques

Sound transmission loss of a wall or partition

We will now determine the way in which sound energy can be transmitted through a wall. This wall could be a partition, the casing of a roller-blind, a tube or any device used to screen the sound source from the space around it. The wall can be defined by its transmission factor t, the ratio between the transmitted power W_2 and incident power W_i. This factor has a value between 0 (soundproof wall) and 1 (sound transparency)

$$t = \frac{W_2}{W_i}$$

The inverse of the transmission factor ($1/t$) expresses the transmission loss of sound by the wall (W_i/W_2), which varies between infinity and 1. In terms of power level, the following is obtained

$$10 \log \left(\frac{1}{t}\right) = 10 \log \left(\frac{W_i W_{ref}}{W_2 W_{ref}}\right)$$

$$= 10 \log \frac{W_i}{W_{ref}} - 10 \log \frac{W_2}{W_{ref}} = L_{W_i} - L_{W_2} = R$$

The sound reduction index R expresses in decibels the inverse of the wall's transmission factor. In the laboratory this index is measured by having separate rooms for emission and reception (Fig. 4.9). R is determined by measuring sound pressure level L_{P_1} and L_{P_2} in the two rooms. As shown in Appendix 3, the following is obtained

$$R = L_{P_1} - L_{P_2} - 10 \log \frac{A}{S}$$

where A is the equivalent absorption area of the receiving room and S is the area of the wall under test.

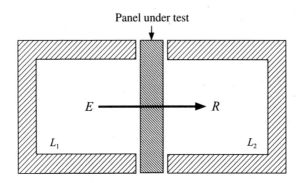

Fig. 4.9 *Measurement of sound transmission loss*

To give an idea of how the sound weakening index of a wall should work, when $R = 30$ dB, a normal conversation in a room can be heard clearly in the adjacent one. If $R = 40$ dB, the conversation is still intelligible. When it is 50 dB, the conversation is still audible but is no longer intelligible. An index of 60 dB is required to block it out almost completely.

The consequence of this is that a reasonable thickness of an absorbent material accounts for very little in the sound weakening index of a wall. In the best of cases, the absorption coefficient reaches 0·9. Should only the porous material be present (and not the wall which supports it and really reflects the waves) then we can estimate that about 5–10% of incident energy would have crossed it. This is far from the 0·000 001 equivalent to 60 dB attenuation which is necessary.

As we will now see, it is essentially the massive character of walls which is responsible for their sound insulation properties from one room to another.

A simple model will show us what happens for a wave propagating perpendicularly to the plane of the wall. The mechanism of energy transmission across the wall is as follows. On the source side, the wall (with surface area S) is submitted to alternating variations of pressure, and therefore to an alternating force which will cause it to oscillate. The acceleration at a unit surface is therefore proportional to incident pressure and inversely proportional to mass. In an oscillating system, velocity of the motion is proportional to the acceleration and inversely so to the frequency. This velocity is therefore proportional to the incident pressure and inversely proportional to the product of mass and frequency. The movement of the wall or partition is transmitted to the air particles in the receiving room. The energy transmitted is proportional to the square of the alternating velocity of the particles: it is therefore inversely proportional to the square of the mass, and to the square of the frequency.

The result of this is the mass law (Fig. 4.10). Expressed as levels this law states

Mass law

The sound loss index increases by 6 dB with each doubling of mass or frequency.

(For a given material, the doubling of mass is obtained by doubling the thickness.)

Example question: 'Knowing that brick 12 cm thick can give a

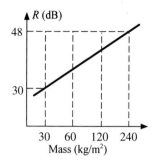
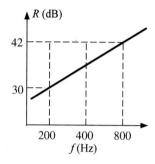

Fig. 4.10 Mass law expressed on logarithmic scales

wall of 240 kg/m^2 with attenuation index at 200 Hz of 48 dB, what will be the attenuation index at 800 Hz of a lead sheet of surface mass 30 kg/m^2?'

Answer: From 240 to 30 kg/m^2, the surface mass is divided by 8: -18 dB. From 200 to 800 Hz, the frequency is 4 times as great: $+12$ dB. The combined effect of these two changes therefore causes a decrease of 6 dB. The value sought is 42 dB, independent in principle from the nature of the material.

Wave–wall coupling: real mass law

Until now, we have considered a displacement under the action of a plane sound wave, propagating perpendicularly to the plane of the wall. Every point of the wall was therefore submitted to the same pressure variation at a given moment. In the case of oblique incident waves, some points of the wall will undergo opposite pressure changes. Fig. 4.11 shows the deformation of the wall, induced by waves approaching from the left, which as before generate in their turn waves in the medium situated to the right of the wall, and in the same direction (for air, this occurs on both sides).

The wall could be considered as consisting of elementary masses that can slide freely in relation to one another, as depicted in Fig. 4.11(b). If this is so, the reasoning used in the previous paragraph leads to the same result, expressed by the

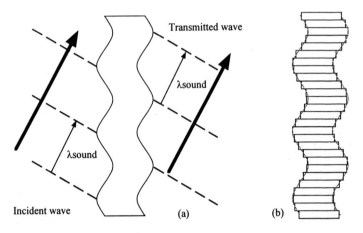

Fig. 4.11   Transmission of (a) oblique incident wave and (b) simplified model

mass law. However, this is not the real situation. Each elementary mass is also linked, with a certain stiffness, to its neighbours. A vibration at one point of the wall propagates as a flexural wave (Fig. 4.12). Generally all flexural waves coming

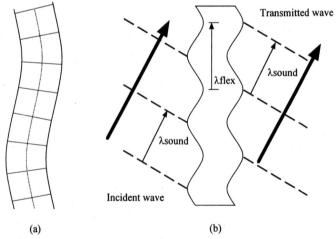

Fig. 4.12   (a) flexural wave; (b) coincident wave

from the different points excited by the sound wave tend to cancel out each other.

However, for some incidence angles θ and frequency f, resonance or significant coupling effects will occur between the incident sound wave and the flexural wave it creates. This coupling will in effect be optimum if the velocity of the trace c' (i.e. the apparent speed) of the sound wave, along the wall, and the speed c_f of the wave in the wall coincide. In these conditions, the sound wave therefore continually reinforces the flexural wave. This is obtained when

$$c_f = \frac{c}{\sin \theta}$$

The coincidence is therefore possible only if $c_f > c$ since a sine is less than 1. Now, the flexion wave speed in a panel depends on the frequency. The frequency f such that $c_f = c$ is the critical frequency f_c of the wall. It is shown that

$$f_c = \left(\frac{c^2}{2\pi h}\right)\left[\left(\frac{12\rho}{E}\right)(1-\mu^2)\right]^{1/2} = \left(\frac{c^2}{2\pi}\right)\left(\frac{m}{B}\right)^{1/2}$$

where c is the velocity of sound in air, h is the wall thickness, ρ is the density, E is the wall's modulus of elasticity (N/m^2), μ the Poisson's ratio; $m = \rho h$ is the mass per unit area and B is the bending stiffness (or coefficient of stiffness per unit length, Nm).

The critical frequency is inversely proportional to the thickness.

In the case of a large steel plate, the critical frequency ranges from about 1 kHz for a 1 cm thickness to 10 kHz for 1 mm. Other typical values of f_c for 1 cm thickness of material are 1·8 kHz for concrete and 6 to 1·8 kHz for wood.

When $f = f_c$ the flexural vibration amplitude gives a strong transmission in the second medium and the weakening index declines noticeably. Fig. 4.13 shows the curve of this index as a function of frequency, in a situation where waves arrive on the wall from all directions (a diffuse field). It is thus shown that behaviour here is governed by the mass law below f_c, whereas

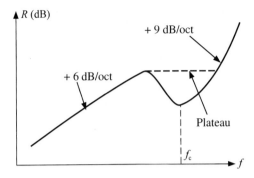

Fig. 4.13   Real attenuation of a wall

above that value it grows by +9 dB/oct. Attenuation is frequently characterized either by a simple plateau or a weak reduction of around f_c.

Double walls

There is a surprising paradox concerning sound (and also heat) illustrated by Fig. 4.14, which leads to the use of double walls. Assume that a wall of thickness h gives an attenuation of 30 dB.

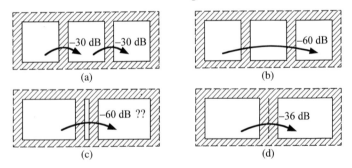

Fig. 4.14   Paradox of a double thickness

In the first set-up represented, the loss observed between the source room and the receiving room is 60 dB (a and b). The idea is to reduce the intermediate room to just a layer of air and thereby hopefully, to preserve an attenuation of about 60 dB (Fig. 4.14(c)). However, if the air layer is removed it amounts to having a partition $2h$ thick between the two rooms: the loss index is therefore $30 + 6 = 36$ dB (Fig. 4.14(d)).

It is therefore highly desirable to have the mass of the wall spread over two panels separated by a thin layer of air, although that arrangement is not really as effective as that shown in Fig. 4.14(c). The air layer filling the cavity between the two partitions acts as a spring which sets up a couple between them and, frequently, a dependent overall behaviour.

At very low frequencies the two panels vibrate in phase: the behaviour is analogous to that of a partition $2h$ thick. For a resonant frequency f_0 they vibrate in phase opposition at very high amplitude. The loss index then sharply decreases and becomes lower even than that of a sole panel. Frequencies higher than f_0 give vibration isolation like a spring-mass system well above its resonant frequency. The loss index then increases rapidly: 18 dB/oct (Fig. 4.15).

In applying a double-facing system the main problem is that of disassociating the two panels. Efficiency of the double wall is increased by placing an absorbent material (mineral wool) in the cavity in order to reduce the undesirable cavity modes.

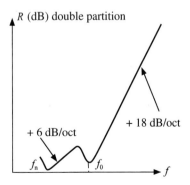

Fig. 4.15   Sound loss of a double wall

Non-uniform walls

Non-uniform walls do not have the same attenuation character-istics over the whole surface S. Assuming that part of the surface S_A presents a high loss index R_A, whereas another portion S_B has a small R_B, what will the resultant index be?

Starting from each index, we calculate the corresponding transmission factors t_A and t_B, by inversing the relation $R = 10 \log(1/t)$. The wall transmission factor is therefore

$$t = \frac{(t_A S_A + t_B S_B)}{S}$$

From this is deduced R, whose value is between R_A and R_B, and the closer the value comes to the smaller index, the greater the difference between the two indices and the larger the surface S_B. When the gap between the two indices is greater than 20 dB the calculation gives the range of figures shown in Table 4.2.

Table 4.2. *Sound reduction index of a two-part wall*

Ratio S_B/S_A: %	1	10	12·5	16	20	25	31·5	40	50	62·5	80	100
$R = R_B$ plus...: dB	20	10	9	8	7	6	5	4	3	2	1	0

This is a surprising result. It shows the extent to which sound, like water under pressure in a duct, is ready to escape at weak points. A speaker cabinet made of a panel with index $R_A = 60$ dB, but having a slit, a hole with $R_A = 0$ dB, on only 1% of the total surface, gives a resultant loss $R_B + 20 = 20$ dB. This value falls to just 10% dB if the opening represents 10% of the surface.

Good sound insulation can be achieved only if the speaker is hermetically sealed.

Lateral flanking transmission

It is only under conditions of complete vibrational isolation of the rooms that transmission from one to the other occurs completely through the wall. In practice, a large proportion of the sound is transmitted when common structures are set in vibration that form phonic or acoustic bridges between rooms, such as ceilings, tiling, adjacent walls, ventilation shafts and piping (Fig. 4.16). One talks of lateral transmission in the first

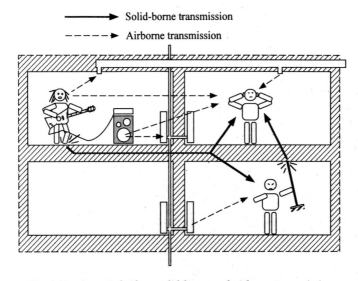

Fig. 4.16 Acoustic bridges: solid-borne and airborne transmission

three cases and intercommunication in the other two. To foil the effects of acoustic bridges requires as much skill as for thermal bridges and application of exactly the same rules, which are now well known.

Airborne and solid-borne transmission

All sound transmission brings into play waves which eventually reach our ears through the air. On the way from source to receptor these waves can be propagated through one or several solid objects, as previously demonstrated, with or without attenuation.

In spite of all the solid materials that intervene in the propagation, this is airborne emission, as soon as the first means of transmission is aerial. For example, the sound of a neighbour's violin lesson in his flat, which sets the nerves on edge, arrives by airborne transmission, even though the sound waves propagate by way of the walls and a badly designed collective heating system. Conversely, if the source generates vibrations which are directly transmitted to the room's structure, which then emits sound waves, we are dealing with solid transmission (structure-borne sound). This is how sound from a ventilation unit, an electric drill, a lift operating mechanism or footsteps is transmitted.

For the receptor there is no difference as in all cases it will pick up airborne sound waves, but the distinction of the two forms of transmission is justified for two reasons, as follows.

Different treatments
The first reason is that the two different modes of transmission imply the use of different treatments around the sound source to limit the propagation, as illustrated in Fig. 4.17. In the case of a

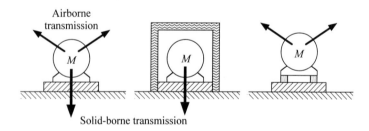

Fig. 4.17 Counteraction of airborne (centre) and solid-borne (right) transmission

motor fixed to the floor, a hood will reduce airborne transmission but will be completely ineffective against solid transmission. Conversely, a viscoelastic suspension will control the latter but have no effect on the airborne transmission.

Different couplings

The second reason for distinguishing the two forms of transmission is the coupling between source and medium. Recall that this term expresses the degree of facility with which the source excites the surrounding medium (the section on Stationary waves and modes in Chapter 2). Generally, this coupling is weak in airborne emission. The power emitted by a given source in air is quite limited, whereas in the case of solid excitation of a resonating structure the source can react by supplying a greater power.

This poor coupling between a solid mechanical structure and air explains, for example, why the displacement of a membrane is several thousand times greater than the movement of air particles which it induces. It also explains why a liquid rather than air is used as an intermediary medium to propagate ultrasound waves used in medical scanning or in lithotripsy (renal calculus destruction).

5

Noise

Sound source, noise source

Noise can be considered as undesirable sound, a definition which conveys how highly subjective is the conception of noise. A marvellous piece of classical music coming from hi-fi speakers will be a quite intolerable noise for the neighbours, if set at maximum volume at three o'clock in the morning.

Generally, noise results from the superimposition of a multitude of sounds, produced most often by a multitude of basic sources having no relation to each other. The amplitude fluctuates and gives the impression of a random phenomenon.

Once again, however, these criteria are highly inefficient. Observation of a sound-level recording on paper cannot possibly distinguish between a symphony and unpleasant sounds. Only an experienced ear can tell the difference.

A pure continuous high-amplitude sound can appear terribly

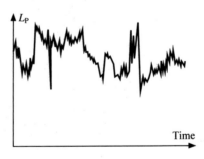

Fig. 5.1   Symphony . . . or cacophony?

noisy. At an equal amplitude, however, it will be tolerated much better than a sound of the same frequency at fluctuating amplitude.

A recording of sound level, like the one in Fig. 5.1, is extremely poor in useful analytical information. It provides no information on which to judge the physiological effects, which depend largely on frequency components, or to determine the sound sources, and therefore no help in treating the causes.

Spectral analysis is the prime tool for analysing a noise source.

Spectral analysis of noise

How accurate an analysis?
Analysers exist that can give, practically instantaneously and highly accurately, the frequency distribution of a signal. However, such devices are only of limited use for an instant analysis of a noise source because the spectral components change incessantly in number, position and intensity, precisely because noise fluctuates. A spectrum can look extremely different from one moment to the next.

However, with prolonged observation averaged over time, in the case of a noise source acting permanently, for example an engine running at constant speed, average levels of the same value will be observed in repeated tests, as long as a whole range or band of frequencies is considered, rather than a single one.

The phenomena can be interpreted when such repeated measures are taken. How then can the band spectrum of a noise source be established?

The range of frequencies in which we are interested is broken down into adjacent bands. We can consider that there is a perfect filter for each band: each filter lets through only those signals corresponding to its band. The energy received at the exit of each filter is accumulated, for a given length of time, for example 10 s. Depending on the degree of accuracy required, a particular number of bands is taken, on the understanding that the higher the number the longer must the measurement be run for the average distribution to be significant. Choice of bands is in accordance with international standards.

Division into octave bands
For division into octave bands the middle frequencies of each band are taken at 125–250–500–1000–2000–4000 Hz, and so on. The end of each band is the middle frequency multiplied or divided by $\sqrt{2}$.

Division into third octave bands
Division into third octave bands, which is more accurate, is commonly used. This type of breakdown is shown in Exercise 3.8 in Chapter 3. We pass from one middle frequency to the next by multiplying it by the cube root of 2, i.e. 1·26. The end of each band corresponds to the middle frequency multiplied or divided by the sixth root of 2: 1·12. Middle frequencies are taken as 20–25–31·5–40–50–63–80–100–125–160–200–250–315–400–500–630–800–1000–1250–1600–2000–3150–4000–5000, and so on.

Figure 5.2 shows spectra represented in two ways. In principle, a noise spectrum should be presented in the form of

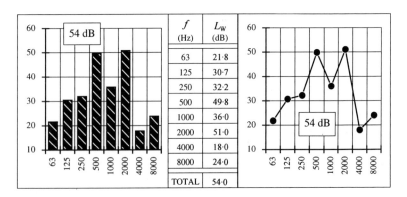

Fig. 5.2   Noise represented as octave band

histograms which, depending on the height of each column, express the sound power contained in each band. Generally, a continuous form is preferred which, although less explicit, lends itself better to superimposition of several spectra for comparisons to be made.

The noise source is therefore equivalent to the superimposition of as many individual sources as there are bands, each with its power level. The reader who is surprised that the overall level (54 dB) is not equal to the sum of the levels of each band should refer to the rules of combination covered in Chapter 3.

Health effects of noise

Time equivalent sound (pressure) level L_{eq}
Sound levels are sometimes measured as intensity (L_I), or more usually as pressure (L_P). For humans or animals the duration of exposure to noise is a highly important factor. At an equal sound power or pressure a noise lasting a few tens of seconds does not have the same effects as it would if it were continuous.

In order to determine the average effects during a given length of time T, of a variable pressure $p(t)$, we find the time-averaged equivalent pressure P_{eq} over the duration considered, and the corresponding level LP_{eq}

$$P_{eq} = \text{Average value of } P(t) = \frac{1}{T} \int P(t) \mathrm{d}t$$

$$L_{eq} = 10 \log \frac{1}{T} \int 10^{L(t)/10} \, \mathrm{d}t$$

The integrals giving the average value are calculated on the time T.

In cases of exposure to very high sound levels caused, for example, by proximity to an airport or motorway or when working with a noisy machine, direct effects are observed on individuals' health or physiology. These effects are compiled in a brochure produced by the French Health Ministry and distributed in France by the Noise Information and Documentation Centre (CIDB).[3] The reader familiar with Molière's language, can refer to the original text but we reproduce here translated extracts, in italics, giving an idea of the orders of magnitude involved. The same figures and information can be obtained from the World Health Organization (WHO) or from the British Department of the Environment (DOE).

Auditory effects

The middle ear is usually damaged by noise only at very high sound level (greater than 120 dB), when the ear drum can be ruptured and the ossicles dislocated. Abrupt changes of pressure on the ear drum (in aircraft, or during deep-sea diving) are also dangerous.[3]

Such damaging modifications of the middle ear therefore generally come from accidental exposure (to an explosion for instance). The inner ear, however, is highly sensitive even to lower levels if these are prolonged

- either by destruction of ciliary cells of the basal membrane, submitted to mechanical constraints that are too strong—a serious, irreversible effect because the cells cannot regenerate.
- or because there is a progressive inhibition of transmission between the cells and the auditory nerve.

Loss of hearing acuteness is usually gradual . . . Although there are great differences between individuals, most studies converge in considering that deafness is very rare when the sound level does not exceed 85 dB(A) for eight hours. This led the European Community to issue, in 1985, a directive obliging employers to inform and protect workers whose daily exposure reaches or exceeds 85 dB(A) or for whom the peak sound pressure reaches or exceeds 135 dB(A).

However, some non-professional activities—pursuits using engines, listening to loud music, shooting—can have the same effect. Workers can protect themselves (with a helmet, earplugs, the hood of a machine etc.) but the situation is different for those who expose themselves voluntarily to sound levels equivalent to those of the noisiest industries (105 dB(A) and over) in discotheques, rock concerts, noisy activities such as clay pigeon shooting, motocross—or even in using their Walkman radio too loud.[3]

Non-auditory effects

Epidemiological and laboratory studies reveal real effects of noise on the general response of the organism (stress) and other sensory systems, but these are difficult to quantify.

The visual system is particularly sensitive since . . . an exposure to noise (98 to 100 dB with a spectrum ranging from 50 to 5000 Hz) is followed by a shrinking of the visual field (by about 10° for red), by less precision in judging depth, a decrease in speed of colour perception and above all a profound change in nocturnal vision.[3]

It is in their interaction with the cardiovascular system that harmful effects of loud noises are the most significant and best quantified. There is a clear correlation between the rate of hearing problems in a population of workers subjected to noises greater than 85 dB(A) and treatment for high blood pressure. Laboratory studies also indicate temporary modifications of heartbeat in the presence of noise.

Noise is also directly responsible for changes in performance, and loss of vigilance (for levels $L_P > 70$ dB). Numerous studies link noise to slow intellectual development in children.

At lower levels we encounter sleep disturbances and psychological and social difficulties provoked by nuisance (neighbourhood problems). Sleep disturbances are a good indicator of the nuisance caused by noise. Outside background noise (measurable inside the house) does not disturb if $L < 40$ dB, with fluctuation lower than 10 dB. In the same conditions, for L between 40 and 50 dB, disturbances are exceptional. However, they become more frequent when fluctuations exceed 10–15 dB, or as soon as the level goes beyond 50 dB.

The European Community Commission estimates that a night level of 30–35 dB(A) inside and peaks of 45 dB(A) do not affect the sleep of normal subjects. The Organization for Economic Co-operation and Development (OECD) recommends, provisionally, that member countries apply regulations such that levels are 35 dB(A) during the period of going to sleep, 45 dB(A) during light sleep and 50 dB(A) during deep sleep . . . The World Health Organization is much more realistic in recommending interior night-time levels of around 35 dB(A).[3]

Prominence

In order to define the nuisance caused by a particular noise more precisely, in relation to the intermittent use of equipment, the notion of prominence has been introduced. Prominence is defined by the difference between the background noise level, which includes the particular noise produced by the considered source, and the residual noise level when this source is switched off. The latter level corresponds to the usual noises as a whole, whether from outside or inside, when the premises are occupied normally and equipment is working as usual.

A decree issued in France (88-523) in 1988, aiming to 'preserve man's health against neighbourhood noise', refers to prominence: this should not exceed 5 dB(A) in daytime (07.00 to 22.00) and 3 dB(A) at night (22.00 to 07.00). However, a correctional term is added to this value, to take into account the fact that the nuisance diminishes if the total utilization time is low. Table 5.1 gives correction factors and tolerated prominences for different utilization times.

Defining sound comfort

It is therefore essential to do everything possible to dampen all sound transmissions in buildings, whatever their source. There are, however, limits that cannot be exceeded, as CSTB acoustics expert R. Josse points out

> The lowest possible background noise level would to all appearances be desirable. In fact, background noise is

Table 5.1 *Prominences tolerated by the French directive 88-523*

Total time of appearance	Correction term: dB(A)	Daytime prominence: dB(A)	Nocturnal prominence: dB(A)
30 s to 1 min	9	14	12
1 min to 2 min	8	13	11
2 min to 5 min	7	12	10
5 min to 10 min	6	11	9
10 min to 20 min	5	10	8
20 min to 45 min	4	9	7
45 min to 2 h	3	8	6
2 h to 4 h	2	7	5
4 h to 8 h	1	6	4
more than 8 h	0	5	3

beneficial: it can mask the little sounds caused by people or equipment in buildings. The lower the background noise the better must be the building's soundproofing against internal noises. In particular, simply abiding by the regulation values for interior insulation does not give satisfactory comfort if the environment is completely silent (in the country).[1]

Interior noises are more difficult to determine than traffic noise outside. They depend largely on the occupants' way of life and their use of the diverse equipment they own. In the end, the dwelling must be designed so that the sound pressure level L_P in a given receiving space does not exceed a threshold, fixed more or less strictly according to the segment of time or the type of occupation of the space, even though emission sources are present

- external to the façade (road noise)
- external to the considered flat (neighbouring flats, communal corridors, equipment outside)
- inside the considered flat.

Regulations tend essentially to coincide in fixing the values corresponding to the first two situations, while different countries have slightly different approaches. The seal of sound comfort, which involves much more exhaustive investigation, also deals with sound emission inside the accommodation. Standardized quantities, which will be encountered later in the text, are defined in the following sections.

Standardized sound isolation
The standardized sound isolation between an emitting room 1 and a receiving room 2 is given by the equation

$$D_n = L_{P_1} - L_{P_2} + 10 \ \log\left(\frac{T_R}{0.5}\right)$$

where L_{P_1} and L_{P_2} are the average sound pressure levels determined in the two rooms and T_R is the reverberation time of the receiving room. The result is calculated using the frequency band. The standardized isolation is just the gross isolation $L_{P_1} - L_{P_2}$, brought down to a standard reverberation time of 0.5 s, which is what can be expected in an average-size furnished room.

The spectral composition of sound emitted in room 1 must be defined and stated. A so-called 'pink noise' is usually taken, which in other words gives the same emission level in all octaves between 250 and 4000 Hz (a 'white noise' gives a level completely independent of frequency). The isolation measured in these conditions is denoted $D_n AT$.

When we determine the sound isolation between the space outside and a room in a house, we refer to road noise. This is much richer in low frequencies than in high frequencies. Its spectral composition for each octave band and in comparison with the level at 1000 Hz is given in Table 5.2. The standardized isolation is therefore denoted $D_n Atr$ when road noise is being considered.

Table 5.2 Spectral composition of a standardized road noise

Frequency: Hz	125	250	500	1000	2000	4000
Sound pressure level L_P: dB(A) compared with the 1000 Hz octave	+6	+5	+1	0	−2	−8

Standardized sound pressure level
In a similar way the standardized sound pressure level can be defined, by fixing T_R at 0·5 s.

$$L_n = L - 10 \log\left(\frac{T_R}{0·5}\right)$$

where L is the sound pressure level in dB(A) measured in the room.

The trends of new sound regulations: French NRA

In *Too quiet an approach to quieter homes*, Susan Traill, editor of *Noise & Vibrations Worldwide*

'finds the UK approach to quieter cities understated in comparison with the more flamboyant and innovative French NRA . . . Noise is a challenge to any bureaucracy as it cuts across many departments. The technical rules tend towards the piecemeal as a result. However, while the French have opted for a framework law, setting no limits for homes and residents and leaving industry to work out how it achieves it, the UK rules concentrate specifically on noise sources and standards connected with materials, equipment and so on.

The UK rules lack the cohesion that the French have established by adopting the principle that homes should be quieter whatever the noise source and the means of reducing noise.'[4]

In a circular published in 1994, the French Ministry of

Housing established the framework of the New Acoustic Regulations (NRA in French), to be applied to all housing construction permit applications from 1 January 1996. They update and supersede the regulations of 14 June 1969 modified on 22 December 1975, and aim to improve significantly the acoustic properties of collective housing, taking into account improvements in building technology and design. A brief guided tour of these NRA measures will be worthwhile.

Specific British regulations will be found in BS 8233:1987 (internal noise in buildings and insulation). In fact, the difference is not so important, and all the figures come mainly from the same recommendations of the WHO.

Noises from outside
The standardized sound isolation D_nAtr in relation to road noise must be a minimum of 30 dB(A), for kitchens as well as main rooms, the value taken with windows closed.

Sound isolation between dwelling units
Between any part of a house or flat, considered as a source room, and a room in another dwelling, considered as a receiving room, the standardized sound isolation D_nAT to airborne noise must be higher than 54 dB(A) if the receiving room is a main (living or sleeping) room, and 51 dB(A) if it is a kitchen or bathroom.

Sound isolation between common passageways and dwelling areas
The values 54 and 51 dB(A) are again encountered. However, they unexpectedly fall to 41 and 38 dB(A) when the common passage or corridor is separated from the receiving room only by a door on to a landing or private passage.

Sound isolation between working premises or garage and living area
In this case, the rule on isolation is more rigorous: 59 dB(A) between working premises and any main dwelling room, 56 dB(A) between a garage (whether individual or collective) and

any main room. These limits fall respectively to 56 and 53 dB(A) if the receiving room is a kitchen or bathroom.

Absorbent covering materials in common passageways
The equivalent area of absorption A of covering materials in corridors and other common passageways must represent at least one-quarter of the ground surface of these passageways.

Impact noises
In a ground-impact test normalized for an impact machine, the standardized sound pressure level L_nAT must not exceed 61 dB(A) in each main dwelling room when impact tests are performed on the floor of areas outside the dwelling (except for outbuildings, balconies and loggias not situated above a main room, common staircases in cases where the building has a lift, and technical installation rooms).

Equipment and installation inside the dwelling
Concerning equipment inside the dwelling, the regulation deals only with mechanical ventilation and heating or air-conditioning plant. With the most usual setting of minimum output, mechanical ventilation must not produce a normalized sound pressure level greater than 30 dB(A) in a main room and 35 dB(A) in a kitchen or bathroom.

For individual heating or air-conditioning units, or for ventilation turned up to maximum output, permitted levels rise to 35 dB(A) in a main room and 50 dB(A) in a kitchen. Kitchens that open on to a main room will be the subject of special texts.

Equipment and installations outside the dwelling
The equipment concerned, outside the dwelling itself, is that which forms collective installations (lifts, boiler room, transformers, water pressurizer, rubbish chutes) and individual equipment coming from a neighbouring dwelling. The levels to be

complied with are again 30 dB(A) in a main room and 35 dB(A) in a kitchen or bathroom of the receiving living area.

In the case of the equipment of a building's mobile envelope (awnings, roller shutters . . .), whose operation time (deployment and retraction) remains less than one minute, a test code stipulates a subtractive correction of 9 dB from the measured level, thereby taking up the spirit of the Ministry's order concerning neighbourhood noises. The effective thresholds are therefore 39 and 44 dB(A) for these products.

Uncertainty

An uncertainty I of 3 dB(A) is applicable to all values previously indicated. I is deducted from all thresholds related to standardized isolations D_n, and added to all thresholds concerning the standardized sound pressure levels L_n.

Improvement of comfort: the Qualitel label of approval

A system of labels exists that classifies the sound comfort, in the same way that a certain number of stars reward good thermal insulation. In France, the Qualitel label gives a dwelling a score, between 1 and 5, after thorough analysis of protection against noise emitted either outside or inside the building. Distinction is made between source and receiving rooms. In each case different types of area are designated: main rooms, wet rooms (bathrooms etc.), passages, circulatory systems, to define the assessment criteria for each score. Equipment, plumbing, boilers and ventilation units are examined as individual pieces of equipment. As collective installations, lifts and garage doors must produce noise of level L_P less than 25 dB(A) if they are to receive the maximum score.

For individual installations outside the dwelling, Qualitel governs only taps and plumbing and wastewater downpipes.

The best score is obtained for a level L_n lower than 30 dB(A) in the main rooms. For individual installations in the interior, only ventilation and heating-air conditioning installations are examined, with a requirement of 30 dB(A) in main rooms, and, at most, 50 dB(A) in the kitchen (if there is a boiler) for the maximum score to be attributed.

In comparison with the New Sound Regulations (for which Qualitel has been a source of inspiration), the label introduces a valuation of the dwelling according to the transmission between the living room and the different bedrooms.

The general method of valuation is instructive as a laudable example of quality assessment. The overall score attributed to a category or to a whole is most often the lowest score found in one of the rooms and not an average score. It is therefore the principle of the weakest link that applies, a particularly relevant one in acoustics.

Noise standard SIA 181

The Swiss standard SIA 181 is the first to cite motorized equipment explicitly for the mobile envelope of buildings in its area of application.

Area of application and interpretation

The standard SIA 181 was registered by the Swiss Standardization Association on 28 May 1988, to come into effect on 1 October of that year. This norm defines in particular the maxima of sound pressure level, with reference to the nature of the premises concerned, the installations and the use to which they are put.

Motorized control systems for the mobile envelope of buildings are directly concerned by the application of this standard, classified as 'technical installations'. They come into the category of products that give rise to so-called non-permanent noise.

In typical usage it is essential to comply with the requirements set out in Table 5.3.

Table 5.3   Maxima imposed by the norm SIA 181

	Daytime 06.00 to 22.00 hours		Night 22.00 to 06.00 hours	
LOW sensitivity Rooms used mainly for practical activities, or by several people, or for short periods only. Examples: workshop, reception room, large offices, canteen, kitchen, sale room, laboratory, corridor . . .	45 dB(A)	50 dB(A)	40 dB(A)	45 dB(A)
COMMON sensitivity Rooms used for intellectual activities, or living rooms, or for sleeping	40 dB(A)	45 dB(A)	35 dB(A)	40 dB(A)
Examples: sitting room, bedroom, classroom, office, singing room, hotel bedroom, hospital ward	F	U	F	U

There are also certain places classed as high-sensitivity areas where users need peace and quiet (for example resting rooms in hospitals and sanatoria, special therapy rooms, music rooms, lecture rooms) for which all levels are lowered by 5 dB(A).

The letter F in the table corresponds to sounds caused by the operation of the installation. The switching on of a device independently of the wishes of the occupant, either because the system is automatic, over which the occupant has no influence, or because it is a device operated in a neighbouring room. U represents noises caused by the user. The device is activated by voluntary action of the user of the room.

Although this is a clear-cut classification it inevitably comes up against cases whose interpretation is not yet settled. Logically, therefore, an automatic switching device, as found in remote control lighting products, saving the user from having to perform the manoeuvre, is classified as U, even if it is not activated directly by the user.

Examples of interpretation

- Open-plan offices in daytime: general operation of blinds controlled by automatic switch—45 dB(A).
- Hospital ward in daytime: general operation of blinds controlled by automatic switch—40 dB(A).
- Bedroom at night: manual operation at will of motorized roller blind—40 dB(A).
- Bedroom at night: operation of motorized roller blind of neighbouring dwelling—35 dB(A).

These values are severe, especially for equipment used for a short time and intermittently, but correspond, as we have seen, to the standard level requirement which will be taken as a reference source in drawing up new European, or even world-wide regulations, based on criteria for sleeping.

Measuring technique

The values shown in Table 5.3 correspond to an evaluation level, denoted L_{rH}. In practice, the measurement made is a measure of the sound pressure level L_P, weighted by curve A, conducted in the room using a sound level meter. The value taken into account is the maximum value measurable, but where the occupant spends most of his time. The measurement so made according to this norm is denoted L_A.

In furnished rooms, L_A must not exceed L_{rH}. For unfurnished rooms, L_A must not exceed $L_{rH} + 3$ dB(A).

Example: all the figures in the table must be increased by 3 dB(A) to compare them with measurements made in new buildings handed over unfurnished but already with finished floor and wallcoverings.

Equipment noise

We have just seen that the determination of the sound pressure at different points in a receiving room is used to evaluate the possible discomfort felt by the occupant, with reference to regulation thresholds. This sound level will, however, depend as much on the position of the measuring points as on the nature of the room itself, its geometry and reverberation properties.

For the same equipment, set up in the same way, but in a room of different geometry or with different coverings, it is impossible to use or extrapolate the foregoing results. Only if the total sound power diffused by the equipment is known can the effects on different types of room or on neighbouring rooms be predicted.

The sound power level L_W is the only objective criterion for comparison between different appliances or installations. It is an overall parameter which, in particular, overcomes the problems of distance from the source and directivity.

The orders of magnitude of the sound power level L_W of equipment are usually higher than the pressure levels measured from the moment the ear is no longer in immediate proximity to the equipment. The reader should not worry about this. These quantities are linked but different.

For household electrical appliances, the working sound power levels measured are as follows and depend on the model (advances in design are tending to reduce these)

- dishwashers: 50–75 dB(A)
- washing machines (5 kg): 50–77 dB(A)
- filtering cooker hood, at fast setting: 50–70 dB(A)
- vacuum cleaner: 60–90 dB(A).

Limit values for appliances and equipment
We conclude this chapter by expressing in figures the sound power of appliances compatible with the regulations just

described. The following equation, demonstrated fully in Chapter 6 (in the section on Sound power measurement), is applied

$$L_P = L_W + 10 \log T_R - 10 \log V + 14$$

where $L_{P;}$ is the level of sound pressure measured by the receptor (in dB), $L_{W;}$ is the level of sound power emitted by the product (dB), T_R is the room's reverberation time (s) and V is the volume of the room in m³.

In Switzerland, a maximum value L_A that does not exceed $L_{P;}$ therefore means

● for a given room, fixing a limit greater than the total sound power L_W diffused by the equipment as a whole
● for a given space volume and equipment, fixing a limit higher than the room's reverberation time (this is done at the architectural design stage, involving the choice of coverings).

The limit will be the easier to comply with the lower the power diffused by the equipment as a whole.

Example 5.1
Consider the unfurnished kitchen of a Swiss flat, where the volume of the room = 30 m³, $T_R = 1.0$ s. It will be occupied between 06.00 and 22.00. What is the maximum sound power of a wall-mounted central heating boiler?

$$L_rH = 45 \text{ dB (switch independent of the user)}$$
$$L_A = 45 + 3 = 48 \text{ dB} \times L_P = L_A = 48 \text{ dB}$$
$$L_W = L_P - 10 \log T + 10 \log V - 14$$
$$= 48 - 10(0) + 10(1.5) - 14 = 49 \text{ dB(A)}$$

(In France the CSTB sets a sound power of below 50–52 dB(A) for such equipment and the figures match reasonably well.)

Example 5.2
Consider a motorized roller shutter in the same kitchen as in Example 5.1.

$$L_r H = 50 \text{ dB (operation by the user)}$$

This time the same calculation leads to a maximum power level (for the part diffused towards the interior)

$$L_W = 54 \text{ dB}$$

Example 5.3
Consider a motorized roller shutter, at night, in a furnished bedroom 30 m^3 in volume, having $T_R = 0.5$ s.

$$L_r H = 40 \text{ dB (operation by the user)}$$
$$L_W = L_P - 10 \log T_R + 10 \log V - 14$$
$$= 40 - 10(-0.3) + 10(1.5) - 14 = 44 \text{ dB}$$

However, for a neighbour occupying an identical room, the transmitted power level must be such that $L_{rH} = 35$ dB, therefore $L_W = 39$ dB.

With account taken of the regulations of sound isolation between rooms (> 50 dB), the level 39 dB in the disturbed room is attained without difficulty if solid transmission does not occur.

Let us now consider the same situation, but in France.

Example 5.4
Take a motorized roller shutter, at night, in a furnished room 30 m^3 in volume, again with $T_R = 0.5$ s.

There is no limit value for the source room

However, for a shutter serving a room in the neighbouring flat it is important that the power diffused towards the receiving room is limited:

L_n 30 (New Sound Regulations) + 9 (corrective term of test code)
$$= 39 \text{ dB(A)}$$
$$L_n = L_P - \log (T_R/0{\cdot}5) = L_P$$
$$L_W = L_P - 10 \log T_R + 10 \log V - 14$$
$$= 39 - 10(0) + 10(1{\cdot}5) - 14 = 40 \text{ dB(A)}$$

We therefore find, to within 1 dB, the same level of requirement for such equipment.

6

Measurement and characterization methods

Measurement of sound pressure

Provided that the level remains under a non-linearity threshold (saturation), a microphone gives an electric signal proportional to the sound pressure, as long as the latter's frequency comes within the operating range of the microphone. This frequency depends essentially on the means of conversion used and on the geometry and mechanical properties of the transducing membrane.

Sound level meters usually incorporate a high-quality microphone, followed by a pre-amplifier, and display the output signal on a voltmeter, with a non-linear recording scale that allows a direct reading of the L_P levels in decibels. An electronic analogue filter device allows readings to be corrected to give values in dB(A). The noise can be measured during a stated time interval and a mean value is displayed (integrating–averaging sound level meter) or in a permanent manner (for instance during the last four seconds) with sliding average and exponential time weighting: the value measured 4 s ago has less influence than the one measured 3 s ago, which is itself less significant than that measured 2 s ago in the averaging process giving the 'instantaneous' value. The more recent models are equipped with means of processing which give an initial spectral breakdown of the signal. Fig. 6.1 shows a model marketed by Bruel & Kjaer, the best known supplier in this field.

Fig. 6.1   Sound level meter (BK2260) (courtesy of Bruel & Kjaer)

The sound level meter is the basic apparatus for quickly estimating the global sound characteristics of an installation, but it is indispensible to have available more powerful devices to undertake detailed signal reading and improvement on a product. Connection of a pre-amplifier output to a spectrum analyser can give a breakdown of the pressure levels by frequency bands (octaves, one-third octaves, narrow option band: one-twenty-fourth octaves). Such information makes possible research on the causes and mechanisms of attenuation of the various spectrum lines present in the signal.

These instruments also have calculation and data-storage capacities. Some manufacturers (such as 01dB^{TM}) offer acquisition modules and processing software that can adapt a fixed or portable personal computer into an analyser (Fig. 6.3).

Fig. 6.2   Analyser (BK2144) (courtesy of Bruel & Kjaer)

Fig. 6.3   'Concerto'—a sound laboratory in a PC (courtesy of 01dB)

Intensity measurement

Capabilities of an intensimeter

The sound intensity expresses the value of the sound power crossing a given surface S, normalized to unit surface area. It is the equivalent of a discharge of energy, or of a power flux, expressed in watts per square metre.

Conversely, the sound power across S is the product of the intensity I_n and the area of S

$$W = I_n S$$

The intensity I_n measured through a sensor of cross-section S, whose orientation is defined by the direction of the normal (perpendicular to the centre) to the surface, is zero if the normal is at right-angles with the power flux, and, conversely, maximum if the normal points in the direction of the power flux. It is in this position that the surface S picks up the maximum power (Fig. 6.4). If I_r denotes this maximum value and θ is the angle between normal n and propagation direction r, we have

$$I_n = I_r \cos \theta$$

An ideal intensimeter could be a sensor with an oriented measuring surface S, and a conversion system indicating the

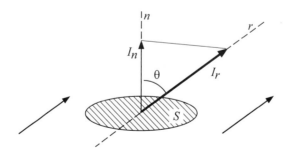

Fig. 6.4   Sound intensity: a vectorial quantity

value I_n, which is positive or negative according to the direction in which energy passes through S.

The utility of such an instrument is founded on three advantages, as follows.

If we position ourselves at any point in space and orient the sensor successively in all directions, the sign of the signal received shows which is the propagation direction. Furthermore, the position of the sensor when the signal is strongest tells the direction of the energy flux. The sources of sound power are therefore detected, by mapping point by point I_r showing (sign), direction and value, as shown in Fig. 6.5.

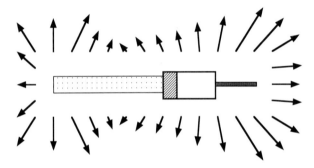

Fig. 6.5   Map of intensity around a complex source

This procedure becomes even more rich in information if one determines, point by point, the frequency spectrum of the signal measured. If this spectrum shows characteristic lines, one can make as many maps as lines and thus define the emission source relative to each one. Fig. 6.6 gives a simplified example in

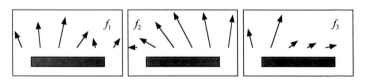

Fig. 6.6   Frequency band map

which the complex source would be characterized by three frequencies, two of which come from the left side, the other from the right.

The intensimetry will also be used to determine the total sound power diffused by a complex source, as demonstrated in the previous paragraph. This time, however, there is no longer a known reverberation room, no T_R, nor correction factors (in the ideal case). How do we proceed?

The source is surrounded by an imaginary surface Σ arranged with a mesh, called the control surface (each square in the mesh has an area equal to that in the sensor), to which we apply the sensor square by square (Fig. 6.7). The sum of the intensities

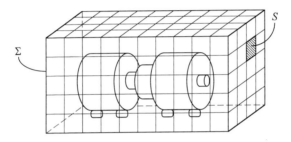

Fig. 6.7   Sound power determination for a source

thus measured, multiplied by the area of Σ, gives the value of the total sound power through Σ, and therefore the power emitted by the source.

The possible symmetries of the source allow the number of effective measurements to be reduced either to one for a spherical source, by taking a surface Σ which is itself spherical, or a single series of measurements if the source has a revolving symmetry (as in tubular motors), by taking a cylindrical surface Σ and displacing the sensor along a generating line of the cylinder.

An even more significant advantage is that the preceding method works for prevailing noises coming from sources outside the volume enclosed by the measurement surface, even if this noise is 10–15 dB greater than the one that has to be measured.

This spectacular property can, for complex installations, lead to individual measurement of the sound power emitted by each sub-unit even if the sub-units function simultaneously. However, Fig. 6.8 shows that each sub-unit must be enveloped by a measurement surface, which is not always possible.

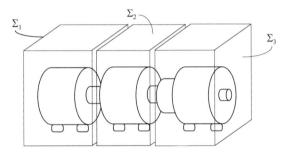

Fig. 6.8   Sound power determination for sub-units

How does this independence from external noise come about? It stems from the fact that the energy fluxes coming from a source outside Σ are counted twice: once negatively when they enter Σ, once positively when they re-emerge. They therefore give rise to a resultant intensity of zero. Fig. 6.9 shows this for a flux perpendicular to the faces of a cubic Σ surface, but it can be

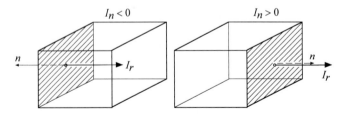

Fig. 6.9   Insensitivity to external sources

generalized to any propagation direction or form of Σ (which in physics constitutes the Gauss theorem).

The only problem raised by the intensimeter (and unfortunately it gives rise to many others) is that of the sensor: it does not exist—at least not in the simple form we would have expected up to now.

The microphone

A microphone possesses a stretched membrane whose vibrations are transmitted to a transducer. This converts the vibrations induced by the alternating pressure $p(t)$ into voltage variations $u(t)$. Therefore $u(t)$ and $p(t)$ are proportional to each other. The transducer element can be a piezoelectric material, a deformable material, a deformable trapped-charge capacitor (electret), or a mobile electric coil in the field of a magnet.

Whatever its type, a microphone is a sensor of alternating pressure. The pressure at a point, inside a liquid or gas, is the same in all directions therefore, whatever the orientation of the surface which measures the effects. A microphone is not at all directional and is not suitable for a vectorial measurement of the sound intensity, as would have been desirable.

Is there no remedy for this? Not completely: we have seen in the section on Directivity of a source in Chapter 2 that there is a close relationship between the size of a source and its directivity. It is the same for sensors: a sensor becomes increasingly directional as its diameter increases to reach and exceed the wavelength λ of the sound waves received. For a sound wave at 100 Hz propagating at 340 m/s, the wavelength is 3·4 m. That is the diameter of the microphone or of the associated reflector needed to capture (to within a few tenths of a degree) the energy flow directions. As Fig. 6.10 suggests, another way should be sought.

The intensity sensor

The sizeable problem mentioned above explains why intensimetry could only really be developed in the 1980s, by taking

Fig. 6.10   Intensimetrus prehistoricus

advantage of great progress in signal processing and computerized calculation methods.

A straightforward observation is at the root of this. With our
two ears, each equivalent to an alternating pressure sensor, and
without extending the outer ear (pinna) to 34 cm diameter, we
succeed in locating a 1000 Hz sound source (Fig. 6.11). What a
single sensor cannot do, two linked to a processing system (the
brain) can more easily achieve.

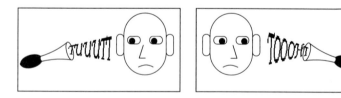

Fig. 6.11   Acceptable natural intensimeter

The sound intensity in a direction r is equal to the average
value (av) of the product of the alternating pressure $p(t)$ and the

component $v_r(t)$ of the alternating velocity of particles in the direction r

$$I_r = (p(t)v_r(t))_{av}$$

A relationship (Euler's equation) exists between the spatial variations of pressure dp/dr and the variations of velocity with time dv_r/dt (the equivalent of Newton's law $F = m\gamma$)

$$\frac{\rho dv_r}{dt} = \frac{-dp}{dr}$$

where ρ is the density of air (or of the gas passed through by the wave). This expression remains true for two sensors neither infinitely close nor very far apart, by a distance of Δr

$$\frac{\rho dv_r}{dt} \simeq \frac{-\Delta p}{\Delta r}$$

where Δp is the difference between the pressures detected at an instant $(p_2 - p_1)$ by the two microphones, that results mainly from the phase differences due to the propagation time, which varies with the signal frequency.

It is possible therefore, starting from this gap Δp, to get back to the value of the particular velocity $v_r(t)$, whereas the arithmetic mean of the signals coming from each sensor gives the pressure $p(t)$. The average value with time of the product of these two quantities gives the intensity I_r.

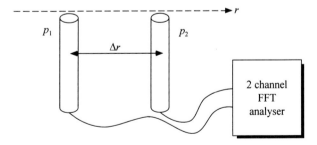

Fig. 6.12   Normal intensimetric probe

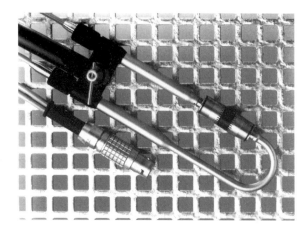

Fig. 6.13   Intensimetric probe (BK3548) (courtesy of Bruel & Kjaer)

This is not perhaps within the grasp of the beginner, who, for extra guidance, needs to be told that the spectral breakdown of I_r, the one which is most useful, is given by the imaginary part of the interspectrum G_{12} of the two signals

$$I_r(f) = \frac{-(\mathrm{imag}(G_{12}))}{(2\pi f \rho \Delta r)}$$

The interspectrum G_{12} is obtained with the aid of a two-channel Fourier Transform analyser (FFT). The courageous reader can turn to references 5–9.

But who would have imagined that all that happens between our two ears? The truth is that it doesn't—the auditory principle is in fact quite different but achieves the same result.

In practice
Although specific equipment exists (B&K^{TM} 3519 or 3548 probe, 2-channel frequency analyser HP^{TM} 3562, PC HP^{TM} 9816, for a typical configuration) and user-friendly software (CETIM IN-TAC), the reader will understand that intensimetric measurements in practice require considerable experience, particularly

Fig. 6.14   Reverberation room (courtesy of CSTB)

to evaluate the method's inherent errors. For instance, perfect calibration of the probes is essential.

For the exact measuring techniques, reference is made to ISO 9614-2 or NF S31-100. Simplifications can occur with symmetrical aspects: in the case of a perfectly axisymmetric arrangement tested in these conditions (as tubular actuators), a series of measuring points on one generating line only of a virtual cylinder Σ coaxial with the tube would be sufficient.

Sound power measurement

Principle
In Chapter 4 it was seen that, in a reverberation room, the sound pressure becomes noticeably independent of the position as

THE TOOLS

soon as the distance from the source is sufficient (diffuse radiation predominates over direct radiation). It is this effect that is exploited to determine the sound power of a piece of equipment, whose emission level is assumed to be constant with time.

Consider a source placed far from the walls of a reverberation chamber: effectively we measure a pressure level L_P which is constant at a good distance from the source and, in particular, identical at any point near the walls.

This level is not reached instantaneously when the source is switched on, but after a time of about T_R, the room's reverberation time (a few seconds). When this sound level stops increasing it means that an equilibrium is reached between the power supplied and the power dissipated (refer to Appendix 2).

The power supplied is what we are going to measure: W, total airborne sound power delivered by the source. The power dissipated is that which is lost at the walls. These are, in fact, not perfectly reflecting (otherwise the reverberation time would be infinite) and are characterized by an absorption coefficient α, and we term equivalent absorption area A (m^2) the product of α and the total area S of the walls. The higher the equivalent absorption area, the greater the source power necessary in order to compensate losses at the walls. In a perfectly reverberating room, the following equation (see Appendix 1), expressed in levels (dB), is obtained:

$$L_W = L_P + 10 \log (A) - 6$$

The absorption area of a room is itself linked to the reverberation time and the volume of the latter by Sabine's law (Appendix 2)

$$A = \frac{0.16V}{T_R}$$

This gives for L_W

$$L_W = L_P + 10 \log (V) - 10 \log (T_R) + 10 \log (0.16) - 6$$
$$L_W = L_P + 10 \log (V) - 10 \log (T_R) - 14$$

From a measurement of the sound pressure level, in the reverberation room where it is constant, the source sound power can be determined, as long as the room's reverberation time is known.

The first correction method: analysis in relation to frequency
The absorption coeffient α is far from being constant for a given wall: it depends on the frequency. The result is that the room's reverberation time T_R has different values in each frequency band. The properties of the reverberation room must be determined beforehand, to find the different values of T_R. This test is conducted by analysing the fall in level, in each frequency band, after abruptly switching off a powerful noise source, or after letting off an alarm pistol.

When the room is then used to define any source, the level L_{P_i} is measured in each frequency band and the power level L_{W_i} corresponding to this frequency is calculated separately. The overall level L_W is obtained by summation (in the sense encountered in the treatment of decibels) of L_{W_i} of each different band.

$$L_W = 10 \log (\Sigma_i\, 10^{0.1\, L_{W_i}})$$

Computerized equipment considerably simplifies acquisition and processing of all these data.

Second correction method: spatio-temporal averaging
The reasoning behind sound power determination assumes that sound pressure does not vary either in time or with distance from walls. To take into account a room's imperfections, a measuring microphone revolving on a silent arm is used or an average over three different points is taken. The test is performed over a sufficiently long time to be able to average the fluctuations with time of the noise emitted by the source.

THE TOOLS

Area of validity
It is important that the equipment whose sound power we want
to measure is, as far as possible, placed in its normal operating
conditions, particularly in the case when the equipment is to be
wall-mounted. The wall will be subject to a different acoustic
load according to whether equipment is suspended in the
middle of the room or put right against the reflecting wall. The
impedance regarding the equipment is different in the two cases
and so the sound power it emits can also be different and is not a
quantity completely dependent on the equipment; akin to an
electric generator whose produced power depends on the
connected load. Measurement must therefore be carried out in
conditions as close as possible to those of a real working set-up.

Moreover, it may be necessary to evaluate the sound power of
an appliance, or conversely predict a sound pressure level from
the sound power, without the ideal conditions of a reverberation
room. This is what we did in the application examples in the
previous chapter.

When the equation relating L_P to L_W is used without taking
into account the direct field emitted by the equipment, is there a
large error? The results of Appendix 1 indicate that the direct
field must be considered if

$$\frac{Q}{(4\pi r^2)} \text{ is not negligible in relation to } \frac{4}{A}$$

where Q is the source directivity factor and r is the distance from
the source (m).

Take Example 5.1 from Chapter 5—a boiler placed against a
wall of a kitchen of 30 m^3, with average reverberation ($T_R = 1$ s)—
and assume that the measurement is taken only 2 m from the
source. In that case

$Q = 2$ (source placed against a reflecting plane surface),

$r = 2$ m, and $A = \dfrac{0.16V}{T_R} = 4.8$ m^2.

The calculations result in a direct-field term one-twentieth as great as the diffuse-field term, which is low enough to be ignored. Even if the boiler were mounted in the corner (effectively a dihedron), increasing its directivity factor ($Q = 4$), the ratio would still be about 10, low enough for the direct field to be rejected in any evaluation.

However, spatial averaging of measurements (by slowly moving the microphone around the room) becomes increasingly necessary as conditions move away from those of an ideal reverberation room.

Standards and documentation
These measuring methods are described in detail in the published standards, for example in the international standards ISO 3740 to 3748, the German ones DIN 45 635 to 45 656 or in the French text NF S 31022 *Determination of the sound power emitted by noise sources*. The standardization texts also specify the various correction terms to apply (for temperature, atmospheric pressure and so on). Measuring equipment manufacturers (Bruel & Kjaer in particular) are helpful in making available their experience and advice by providing training and technical manuals.

Vibration measurement

The sound power W_r radiated by a vibrating plate of surface area S is proportional to the average value over time and space (at any point on the plate) of the square of the vibration velocity

$$W_r = \rho_0 c < (v^2)_{av} > S\sigma$$

where we find the density ρ_0 of air and the speed c of sound in air, the product of which, $\rho_0 c$ ($= 400$) is the sound impedance in air. σ is the plate's radiation factor (see Appendix 4). The index av is used here to express the mean value in time, and the spatial average of X is denoted by $<X>$.

The mean value in time of a square quantity is equal to the square of what is called the effective value of this quantity or *rms* value (root–mean–square). For velocities this gives

$$(v^2)_{av} = v^2_{rms}$$

then

$$W_r = 400 < v^2_{rms} > S\sigma$$

The velocity is measured using an accelerometer placed on the plate, connected to an integrating circuit, and must be taken as an average of the whole surface of the plate. Levels are represented by reference to a plate of unit surface area and radiation factor, so that

$$W_{ref} = 400(v_{rms})_{ref^2}$$

The choice of $W_{ref} = 10^{-12}$ watt affects that of the reference level as effective velocity :

$$(v_{rms})_{ref} = 5 \times 10^{-8} \text{ (unit: m/s)}$$

and velocity level L_V is defined by

$$L_V = 20 \log (v_{rms}/(v_{rms})_{ref})$$

As a result one can write for a vibrating plate

$$L_{W_r} = L_V + 10 \log (S) + 10 \log (\sigma).$$

New methods in development

Methods taking advantage of new opportunities presented by available calculation systems are now being used for certain measurements, for both sound and vibrations.

Cepstral analysis
Developed in laboratories and exploited by engineers at Bruel & Kjaer in the 1980s,[10] cepstral analysis can detect wear or defects

in rotating systems. In reduction gearing a signal is normally obtained whose spectrum reveals only the meshing frequency and its various harmonics. The meshing frequency f_e expresses the number of contacts per second; it is the rotation frequency of a wheel (in relation to another assumed to be fixed), multiplied by the number of teeth. The strength of harmonics of f_e depends on the tooth dimensions. The better designed the tooth profile the smaller the amplitude of all these bands.

When there is a defect in just one of the teeth it is reproduced periodically, not at the meshing frequency but at the rotational frequency f_r of a wheel in relation to another. This defect induces modulation of amplitude or frequency of the resultant signal, which is expressed in the spectrum by the appearance of new lines, shifted symmetrically from the principal lines produced by the meshing alone. The shift is a multiple of f_r.

Figure 6.15 shows what would be obtained in the ideal situation in the case of a single defect affecting a reduction gear with just one stage.

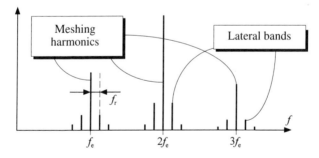

Fig. 6.15   Ideal spectrum of signal from reduction system with defect

All the information on defects is therefore contained in the side bands. The problem is that their amplitude is generally much too small (fortunately) not to be masked by the width of the principal lines. How then can the meshing lines be more clearly separated from the modulation lines?

The idea is to produce the spectrum of the spectrum! Such a procedure reveals, as single lines, the periodical features of the spectrum, more or less hidden in the latter. The spectrum of a temporal signal gives, on a graduated frequency scale (the inverse of time), lines representing the periodic components of the signal. The spectrum of the spectrum gives therefore, on a graduated time scale (the inverse of frequency), lines representing the periodic components of the spectrum.

Let us take the previous example of Fig. 6.15 and fix the values $f_r = 100$ Hz, 20 teeth, which gives $f_e = 2000$ Hz. Having produced the spectrum of the spectrum we obtain a single line representing the meshing periodicity, at $1/f_e$ or 0.5 ms, and a single line representing the periodicity of the defect, at $1/f_r$ or 10 ms—greatly shifted from the preceding one (Fig. 6.16).

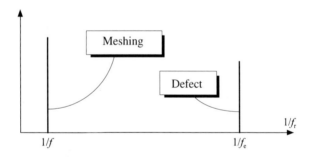

Fig. 6.16   Cepstrum of spectrum in Fig. 6.15

The effect of line separation is reinforced further if the high-amplitude lines, corresponding mainly to the known part, are suppressed in favour of the low-amplitude lines which are usually masked. All that is needed is to take the spectrum of the logarithm of the spectrum, rather than the spectrum of the spectrum directly.

The inventors of this method have humorously called the inverted spectrum, the 'cepstrum', the inverse temporal values of frequency 'quefrency' and still with a straight face specify the 'rhamonics' that appear in complex cepstra.

We should however guard against finding all the advantages in cepstral analysis, which reveals its limitations when applied to multiple reduction gears or those with few teeth per wheel.

Dynamic transmission error

Dynamic transmission error (DTE) can be defined as the instantaneous value of the shift observed between an output quantity (acceleration, velocity or angular position of the shaft) and the value this quantity would have if the transmission was perfect.[11]

In a real transmission the development of DTE with time appears completely chaotic. However, although the signal itself cannot be used, when processed useful information can be obtained on the quality of the transmission

- in terms of amplitude, the typical shift of DTE, measured for all possible values of the average rotation velocity, brings out for some velocities, peaks which express a periodic variation of the tightness of the mesh
- in terms of frequency, spectral analysis of DTE reveals numerous harmonic lines whose amplitude indicates the extent of the defect and whose frequency can point to its source.

Phonoscopy

Phonoscopy is a holographic measuring technique (to simplify we say interferential) elaborated at the CSTB since 1989[12] to obtain wall sound transmission images, giving a much finer appreciation of the events (and of sound losses) than the overall characterization test seen in section on Sound less on a wall or partition in Chapter 4.

The holographic reconstruction uses a breakdown of the sound field into plane waves to allow wave-by-wave analysis of events. In particular, the flexure waves of the plane structure can be extracted and it is possible to determine the corresponding amplitude for each mode (m, n) of the plate. Fig. 6.17 shows the image of the sound energy diffused by a PVC-framed window with double glazing and a roller shutter casing.

Phonoscopy is a laboratory method, restricted to determining the properties of walls, not of sources, since the excitation has to be completely mastered.

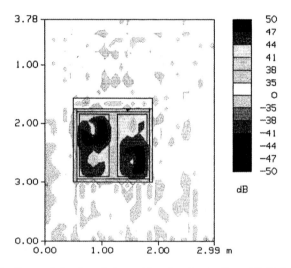

Fig. 6.17   Transmission by window with roller shutter (from CSTB document)

Future methods
There is no doubt that the spectacular progress in studies on deterministic chaos phenomena and constant advances in theory of signal processing, will give rise to new methods to characterize the sources of noise or vibrations in much greater detail.

The application to this type of research of numerous military developments, on electronic scanning antennae for example, opens the way to a practically unlimited field of investigation.

This is greatly assisted by the increasingly common occurrence of electronic components specialized in signal processing (DSP) and by the reduction in arms programmes which stimulate welcome redeployment of efforts.

7

Viscoelastic suspensions and transmissions

Advantage of viscoelastic suspension or transmission

We have at our disposal a machine that generates vibrations

- characterized by variations δF_1 of contact forces on the attachment points to the support
- or with variations δT_1 of the torque transmitted on the rotating shaft
- or with both types at the same time.

These alternating variations superimpose on the static contact force F_1, corresponding for example to 1/4 of the weight of the equipment if it rests in an equivalent way on four supports, or to the static torque T_1 prevailing when a motor is working continually.

A rigid attachment of the equipment to the support, or between the driving and driven shaft, would completely transmit the variations δF_1 or δT_1, and the associated vibration power. This is what happens in Fig. 7.1.

A shrewd move is to place between the attachment points and the support a unit with one or more springs and dampers to hold the mass M of the equipment: viscoelastic suspension (Fig. 7.2(a)). Similarly, a spring-damper unit is put between the output and the driven shafts to provide viscoelastic transmission (Fig. 7.2(b)). In both cases the objective is to have as output (that is on the support, or on the driven shaft) a transmitted

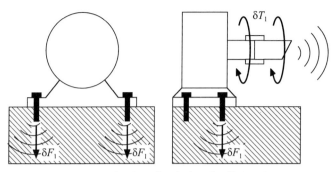

Fig. 7.1 Propagation of variations in effort or torque

alternating force δF_2, or a transmitted alternating torque δT_2 with much smaller amplitude than δF_1 or δT_1.

Viscoelastic transmission or suspension are treated in the same way. In the second case, the forces are replaced by the moments of the forces or the torque and the masses by the moments of inertia.

The coefficient of transmission or transmissibility T_F equal to the ratio $\delta F_2/\delta F_1$ is calculated by writing that the force transmitted to the support is, as an absolute value, equal to the force opposing the movement of the suspended mass M, or the sum

- of an elastic force, proportional to the spring stiffness K and to the displacement of the mass away from the equilibrium position
- of a viscous friction force, proportional to the mass displacement velocity; the proportionality coefficient is the viscous resistance R of the damping system.

If f_n is the natural oscillation frequency of the mass-spring system without damping, the damping ratio ε can be shown to be linked to the viscous resistance by (see references 2, 13, 14 and the sections on Damping and Forced oscillations and resonance in Chapter 1)

$$\varepsilon = \frac{R}{(M4\pi f_n)} = \frac{R}{2KM}$$

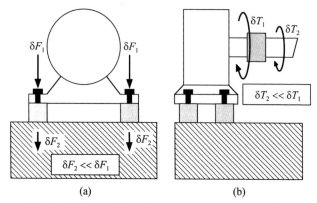

(a)   (b)

Fig. 7.2   Effects of viscoelastic suspension and transmission

The following expression is obtained for the force transmissibility

$$T_F = \sqrt{\left\{ \frac{1 + \left(\frac{2\varepsilon f}{f_n}\right)^2}{\left[1 - \left(\frac{f}{f_n}\right)^2\right]^2 + \left(\frac{2\varepsilon f}{f_n}\right)^2} \right\}}$$

This equation can be applied both to fluid shock absorbers and to the various dampers where elastomers are used. In the latter case the same material provides simultaneously elasticity and damping. The model of elastomeric materials (hysteretic model) makes it appear that the damping ratio is not constant with frequency, whereas that is practically the case for fluids. For these materials ε is inversely proportional to the frequency

$$\varepsilon = \frac{\varepsilon_0 f_n}{f}$$

If we take account of this property, the expression for T_F is simplified and becomes

$$T_F = \left| \sqrt{\left\{ \frac{[1 + (2\varepsilon_0)^2]}{\left[1 - \left(\frac{f}{f_n}\right)^2\right]^2 + (2\varepsilon_0)^2} \right\}} \right|$$

The value $2\varepsilon_0$ corresponds to the material's loss factor η (see Appendix 4).

Figure 7.3 gives curves for T_F as a function of the excitation frequency f, for four different values of the damping ratio. The horizontal axis shows the excitation frequency expressed as a function of the natural frequency. The vertical axis is logarithmic.

Unlike the result that would be obtained in fluid damping, the resonant frequency f_r is always equal to f_n. Moreover, the curves can confirm that the transmission T_F is equal to the inverse of $2\varepsilon_0$

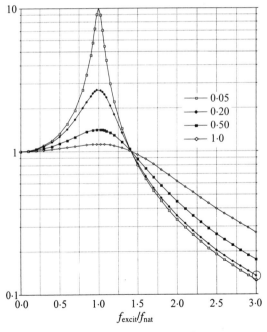

Fig. 7.3 Curves for the force transmissibility of an elastomeric system

when $f = f_n$, and when ε_0 is quite small. In this case

$$\text{if } f \gg f_n, \text{ then } T_F \simeq \frac{1}{\left[\left(\frac{f}{f_n}\right)^2 - 1\right]}$$

Our problem is now the following: for given equipment and excitation frequency, how can the size of the viscoelastic suspension be determined?

Choice of the natural frequency

It is, of course, important that the excitation frequency f used in our calculations (the lowest of the vibration frequencies generated by the equipment) should be very high compared with f_n and, more exactly, compared with $1 \cdot 4 f_n$, in order to be situated in an area of high damping.

As an example, if the suspension dimensions are chosen so that the natural frequency is equal to one-third of the lowest excitation frequency, f, and if the damping ratio is $0 \cdot 2$, the transmission is about $0 \cdot 13$ (the encircled point on the curves in Fig. 7.3). Therefore, 87% of the alternating force is eliminated. This is already quite good, but why not do better?

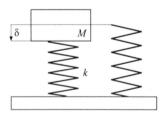

Fig. 7.4   Static deviation δ

Application of the formula giving T shows that if the natural frequency is now taken as one-thirtieth of f the result is 100 times better than previously: $0 \cdot 0013$, the ideal, to eliminate the vibrations. (As soon as $f \gg f_n$ T decreases with the square of f.)

The lowest value for f_n will give the best results in damping at low frequencies. How can we reduce f_n?

$$f_n = \frac{1}{2\pi}\sqrt{\frac{K}{M}}$$

As the mass M of the equipment is given, there is little other choice than to reduce as far as possible the stiffness K of the spring—and therefore to admit a large deflection (compression) δ of the latter under the effect of the static charge F_e.

Any variation in the nominal value of M, or any extra static force, will be expressed by a large, very likely unacceptable displacement of the equipment. For example, the tube of a motorized roller shutter on an elastic suspension could rise ten or so centimetres just because the mass M diminishes when the slats pile up during the closing phase.

That is not the only problem. Let us assume that we stoically put up with the inconvenience mentioned, and that we choose a very small value of f_n: 1 Hz for example. All the windows on the corridor side are equipped as soon as possible with suspensions according to this principle. Imagine the scene in the office. It's time for tea, which is brought by a young lady treading emphatically in her high heels, pounding the floor at the fatal rhythm of one step per second. The rolling tubes start to shake, then wriggle and stamp, and finally make a break for freedom, breaking hinges, brackets and corner pieces. This is the nightmare vision for all manufacturers and installers, who would have very little chance of being consulted a second time for this important renewal contract.

We should therefore hold back our ambitions on the choice of a small value of f_n, and be reassured. The disaster described can still only happen in films. In practice f_n will be about 10 Hz.

In addition, for a chosen value of f_n, it will be best to double simultaneously the stiffness K of the suspension and the value of the mass M. We will then have the same natural frequency, the same attenuation for transmitted alternating force, but a motion amplitude of half the value.

In the case of elastic suspension, using a real spring, there is a very simple relation between the natural frequency f_n and the static deflection (compression) δ caused by the weight of the equipment.

For a single spring

$$F = P = Mg = K\delta$$

where $g = 9 \cdot 81$ m/s^2, therefore

$$f_n = \frac{1}{2\pi}\sqrt{\frac{K}{M}} = \frac{1}{2\pi}\frac{g}{\delta} = 15 \cdot 8\sqrt{\frac{1}{\delta}}$$

which gives f_n in Hz if δ is in mm. Conversely, with these units

$$\delta = \left(\frac{15 \cdot 8}{f_n}\right)^2$$

For example, a natural frequency of 10 Hz will be obtained by choosing elastic materials (springs or others as long as they behave linearly) such that, under loading, they are compressed to 2·5 mm. This value is perfectly acceptable.

Choice of the damping rate

To reduce transmission as much as possible in the attenuating area of operation, it is necessary to have the weakest damping possible, even none at all. This time it is the transitory regime, linked to the starting up or switching off of the equipment, which imposes a serious limitation. In a starting phase the equipment necessarily generates a frequency that grows, before reaching its operational frequency, passing through the resonant frequency on the way with all consequences.

This effect is the temporary but inevitable counterpart of the gains acquired once normal frequency is reached. It is essential to minimize it by employing materials with damping coefficients high enough to withstand the resonant phase in the transitory regime. This constraint does not, however, pose many problems, since the damping is much more sensitive in the resonant zone than in the attenuation zone. In practice, an ε of about 5–10% will be chosen.

Adaptive and active suspensions

Like the constraints on ε already mentioned, those on f_n have inspired the development of electrically controlled, alterable stiffening and damping systems. This is the principle of adaptive suspensions, whose use is particularly pertinent for cars, where different frequencies must be filtered out depending on speed and terrain. It is easier to arrange mechanical action on damping than on stiffening, by modifying the circulation of damping fluid using quick-response valves. This is the technique used in hydroactive suspensions, in which one or two diversion circuits act in parallel on the piston, with electric vanes of response time about 20 ms. The so-called electro- or magneto-rheologic fluids are likely candidates for future generations of equipment. Adaptive suspension therefore consists of modifying as far as possible the parameters of a passive suspension, which requires little energy in relation to the vibration energy.

The real active suspension consists of having one or several activators, governed in a closed loop by a servocontrol, which keeps the structure around its rest point in spite of the disturbances caused by vibrations. The chain therefore also includes one or more vibration sensors and the activators must be powerful enough to counteract the vibration system they have to suppress. The energy spent is therefore at least equal to the vibration energy to be opposed. Design problems (or the cost) of activators mean that active suspensions are still not attractive for large-scale applications. Piezoelectric ceramics or polymers (PVDF) or magnetostrictive materials (Terfenol-D^R) are used.

Degrees of freedom of the suspended system

When suspended, equipment has in fact six degrees of freedom. For the suspensions, three modes of translation are distinguished: vertical, transverse horizontal and longitudinal horizontal. There are three modes of torsion: pitching, yawing and rolling—as shown in Fig. 7.5.

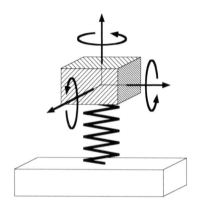

Fig. 7.5   Not one but six degrees of freedom

Each of these movements, induced on the equipment by a force F_{1v}, F_{1th}, F_{1lh}, or a torque T_{1p}, T_{1l}, T_{1r}, will give rise to a vertical transmitted force, the sum of which gives the total force F_2 transmitted by the suspended equipment to its support.

There is a good reason therefore to combine the different transmission curves associated with each of these modes. Omitting to combine the curves can lead to disappointing experimental results, if only due to the fact that the mode not taken into account gives rise to a natural frequency for the suspension much higher than the calculated one (Fig. 7.6).

In particular we will avoid natural frequencies of other modes, situated above f_n of the vertical mode, by ensuring that the system's horizontal stiffness is at least as low as its vertical stiffness.

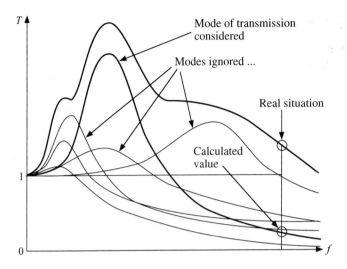

Fig. 7.6 Combination of different modes

It is also recommended to avoid the excitation of undesirable modes, that the line of action of the alternating force passes through the system's centre of gravity, which must be set as low down as possible, at the best position corresponding to the median plane of the elastic supports, as shown in Fig. 7.7.

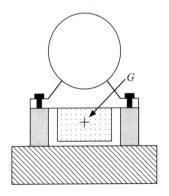

Fig. 7.7 Ideal position for centre of gravity

151

Influence of the support

All that has just been seen assumes a rigid, immobile and non-deformable support. This is not always the case, which creates many surprising results.

Think of a motorized reduction unit placed in a casing (box) and attached to it at a fixed point by a viscoelastic suspension to attenuate the transmission of vibrations. The casing is also attached firmly to a support asssumed to be rigid and of infinite mass (a concrete wall or floor for example).We therefore have a double mass-spring system as set out in Figs 7.8 and 7.9

- the motor-box unit has a transmission $T_1 = \delta F_b / \delta F_m$
- the box-wall assembly has transmission $T_2 = \delta F_w / \delta F_b$
- and the resultant transmission is the product $T = T_1 T_2$.

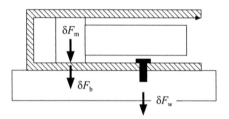

Fig. 7.8   Hazardous arrangement: separation of motor–casing and casing–wall attachment points

It is therefore a coupled oscillator that is functioning here, whose behaviour is defined in the following.

If M_2 were fixed, the natural frequency of M_1 would be given by the expression

$$f_a = \frac{1}{2\pi} \sqrt{\left(\frac{K_1}{M_1}\right)}$$

an equation which serves as a basis for establishing the dimensions of the elastic suspension, if the movement of the casing is ignored.

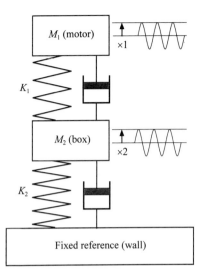

Fig. 7.9   Situation shown in Fig. 7.8

Assuming that the motor M_1 is fixed, this time the natural frequency of casing M_2 can be defined

$$f_b = \frac{1}{2\pi} \sqrt{\left[\frac{(K_1 + K_2)}{M_2} \right]}$$

because the mass M_2 is then submitted to two elasticities K_1 and K_2.

When the whole problem is solved, a coupling term then emerges with a frequency f_{ab}

$$f_{ab} = \frac{1}{2\pi} \sqrt{\left[\frac{(K_1 + K_2)}{\sqrt{(M_1 M_2)}} \right]}$$

and it is shown that in fact two resonances are present, with the frequencies f_r (f_{r1} and f_{r2}) calculated from the following rather user-unfriendly expression

$$2f_{r^2} = (f_{a^2} + f_{b^2}) \pm \sqrt{[(f_{a^2} - f_{b^2}) + 4f_{ab^4}]}$$

153

Table 7.1 *Six examples of configurations and their effect on resonances*

1	$K_2 = 0$ $M_1 = M_2$	$f_b = f_a$ $f_{ab} = f_a$	$f_{r1} = 0$ $f_{r2} = 1.4f_a$	$x_2 = x_1$ $x_2 = -x_1$
2	$K_2 = K_1$ $M_1 = M_2$	$f_b = 1.4 f_a$ $f_{ab} = f_a$	$f_{r1} = 0.6f_a$ $f_{r2} = 1.6f_a$	$x_2 = 0.64x_1$ $x_2 = -1.56x_1$
3	$K_2 = 3K_1$ $M_1 = M_2$	$f_b = 2f_a$ $f_{ab} = f_a$	$f_{r1} = 0.8f_a$ $f_{r2} = 2.1f_a$	$x_2 = 0.36x_1$ $x_2 = -3.4x_1$
4	$K_2 = 3K_1$ $M_1 = 4M_2$	$f_b = 4f_a$ $f_{ab} = 1.4f_a$	$f_{r1} = 0.9f_a$ $f_{r2} = 4.03f_a$	$x_2 = 0.19x_1$ $x_2 = -1.5x_1$
5	$K_2 = 0$ $M_1 = 0.5M_2$	$f_b = 0.7f_a$ $f_{ab} = 0.7f_a$	$f_{r1} = 0.44f_a$ $f_{r2} = 1.14f_a$	$x_2 = 0.8x_1$ $x_2 = -0.3x_1$
6	$M_1 \ll M_2$	$f_b \ll f_a$ $f_{ab} \ll f_a$	$f_{r1} = 0$ $f_{r2} = f_a$	$x_2 = 1$ $x_2 = -0$

Furthermore, the amplitude of the casing movement x_2 is given by

$$x_2 = x_1 \left[1 - \left(\frac{f_r}{f_a} \right)^2 \right]$$

Using examples in Table 7.1 and Fig. 7.10, it can be affirmed that the coupling pushes apart the resonant frequencies of the system as a whole, to either side of the individual values of the natural frequencies. This effect becomes more pronounced the closer the frequencies are together. Because of this

(a) the natural frequency of the whole is not the same as the one predicted by the calculation for the suspension
(b) transmission to the rigid support is much greater than expected
(c) for certain excitation frequencies, the mass M_2 will take on a non-negligible motion . . . and itself become an important noise source.

These drawbacks are avoided by retaining solutions such that $f_b \ll f_a$ ($f_b \simeq f_a/10$)

- by choosing the greatest possible mass for the casing
- by choosing for the casing a material of the smallest possible stiffness (e.g. for the same mass, PVC is better than steel).

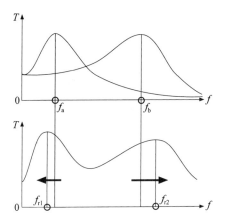

Fig. 7.10   The coupling term spreads the resonances apart

Maximum effort will be made to eradicate the problem by having the same attachment point for the casing to the rigid structure and for the motor to the casing.

If, however, the support structure is not itself rigid (a partition for instance), the procedure has to be started again, but introducing the parameters K_3, M_3 and ε_3 for the partition, to evaluate its behaviour.

Choice of viscoelastic materials

Viscoelastic material
In these applications concerning light equipment for buildings, it is not necessary to resort to springs and oil-damped shock absorbers. There exists a whole range of rubber (neoprene)

materials and elastomers that represent simultaneously an elastic property, therefore a stiffness K, and a damping of about the required degree. For example a rubber with 40 Shore Hardness has a relative damping rate of 0·02 (4 times as high as steel). Natural rubbers have the drawbacks of ageing badly and of being sensitive to attack (by oils and ultraviolet (UV) light for instance). Much more practical injectable elastomers are now available (thermoplastic elastomers, TPE). The elastomer should always be treated to eliminate sensitivity to UV light.

In all cases the material must be used in compression and not under tension, which implies a prestressed condition which is often natural in viscoelastic suspension design.

If the material has non-linear properties, its dynamic characteristics are not determined by the value of its static deflection, but by the slope of the property giving this deflection as a function of the force applied. The value of δ to consider is then what we call the subtangent (Fig. 7.11).

This non-linearity effect is not strong for rubbers, but becomes more marked in certain polymers (e.g. Hytrel[R], Santoprene[R]).

Note in passing that the non-linearity when F is high allows self-limitation of high-level deformations, which is very useful when the system passes through resonance.

Graphic method

The equation giving transmission as a function of frequency is considerably simplified in the case where the damping ε is weak enough for us to ignore the terms in ε^2. As already seen, in the zone $f > f_n$

$$T_F \simeq \cfrac{1}{\left[\left(\frac{f}{f_n}\right)^2 - 1\right]}$$

which in turn gives

$$f_n \simeq \frac{f}{\sqrt{\left(1 + \dfrac{1}{T_F}\right)}}$$

From this expression can be traced, on the diagram giving f_n as a function of the excitation frequency f, the locus of the values for a given transmission T_F, therefore for a required attenuation $(1T_F)$. From the desired attenuation and the excitation frequency, the natural frequency is derived, hence also the suspension stiffness and even the subtangent δ. The relation between f_n and δ can give a direct scaling of the axis f_n with subtangent values. The graph is drawn on logarithmic scales (Fig. 7.12).

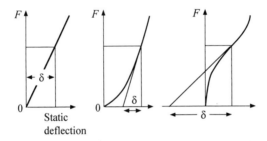

Fig. 7.11   Linear and non-linear response materials

On the graph it can be checked that everywhere $f_n = f/2$ for $T_F = 1$, and that f_n is close to $f/10$ when $T_F = 0.01$.

Example of use in practice
Assume that it is necessary to eliminate 90% of the vibrations occurring at 50 Hz. The compression (if the material behaves linearly) or the subtangent (if non-linear) can be taken directly from the graph (Fig. 7.12), usually supplied by the manufacturer, in this case 1 mm. Calculation by the formula already given leads to the same result:

$$T_F = 0.1 \qquad f_n \simeq 50/\sqrt{11} = 15.1 \text{ Hz} \qquad \delta = (15.8/15.1)^2 \simeq 1 \text{ mm}$$

157

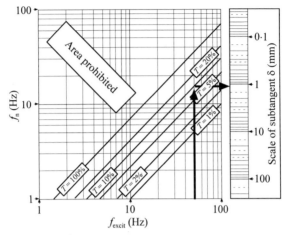

Fig. 7.12   Graphic determination of the subtangent required

Example of suspension and transmission design

Vertical bracket 1

Figure 7.13 shows a possible viscoelastic suspension in the case of a brace supporting an axial motor and fixing it to a vertical panel. The attenuation required here is that of the horizontally transmitted vibrations. The upper and lower parts of the suspension show contrasting behaviour in response to horizontal forces. Compression occurs in the right-hand part of the upper elastomer, in the lower part of the lower elastomer. However, both are subject to the same constraint of shearing. An additional prestress is ensured by screwing the whole unit against the wall, as extensional tendencies of non-compressed components will then be prevented. Care must be taken to ensure that this additional compression is kept within the elastic limit and it must not be accounted for in δ, which is what is induced by the suspended mass.

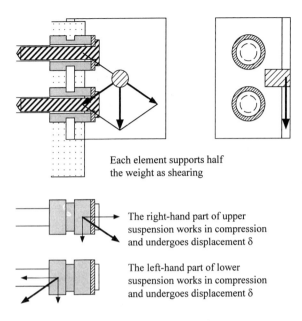

Each element supports half
the weight as shearing

The right-hand part of upper
suspension works in compression
and undergoes displacement δ

The left-hand part of lower
suspension works in compression
and undergoes displacement δ

Fig. 7.13   Vertical brace attachment 1

Vertical bracket 2
In order to resolve the same problem of fixing, it may be advantageous to fit a device which avoids shearing of the viscoelastic parts. Fig. 7.14 shows the principle of such an arrangement.

Viscoelastic transmission
Figure 7.15 gives an example of a viscoelastic coupling. The geometry and specification of the material are chosen such that the elastic domain remains in force.

Further information
The information and effective assistance necessary in this highly complex field can be obtained from the manufacturers. An exhaustive list will be found in the international directory of

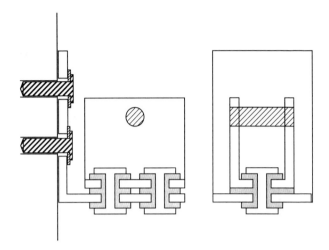

Fig. 7.14   Vertical brace attachment 2

Noise and Vibrations Worldwide (see Useful addresses at the end of the References). References 13 and 14 give complete coverage of insulation against vibration.

Fig. 7.15   Viscoelastic transmission (from SOMFY document)

Part two　Improvement

8

From motor to building

Considerable potential advantages

This short chapter introduces the steps which can be taken to improve performance, now that we have at our disposal tools which enable us to understand the phenomena involved and to find appropriate solutions to any problems.

We have to ensure that our actions solve a real problem. As an example, let us take an item marginal to building services, at least for the quantities involved, but typical of the requirements that have developed: projection screens such as those installed in classrooms, conference halls or lecture theatres. Their construction is similar to many roll-up interior screens and sun blinds.

A marketing approach will give a better feel of the way buyers' expectations of these motorized products have evolved.

For the building services manager, motorization gives the principal advantage of ease of maintenance: the motor ensures regular movement without undue force, which considerably prolongs the life of the equipment. Manually-operated systems, although simple and efficient, with straps, chains and cords or rails, are ill suited for many different users, often with no time to spare. The fact that the screen (made of costly material) is motorized should ensure that it is always rolled up after use, away from dust and other harmful agents. The building manager will normally decide to invest in this kind of equipment—but what will the user think?

Except in rare cases, it is not the saving of physical effort by motorization which is attractive, rather the ability to continue one's lecture without a break in audience attention when operating the screen. It is therefore essential that noise distraction is not added to the inevitable visual distraction caused by the screen's movement. Freed from having to manoeuvre it himself, the lecturer will be less tolerant of noise from the product, a less important aspect when all his attention was taken in manual operation! This applies to most users of motorized products.

As stated in the Introduction, the first motorization amounted simply to the attachment of an electric actuator on to a conventional product designed for manual operation, dramatically altering its behaviour as far as vibration is concerned.

Several motorized projection screens on the market have been tested by SOMFY and the CSTB. Let us take one as an example a screen of a common size (2 m × 2 m). The screen (Fig. 8.1) consists of a functioning part: the rolling tube and its fixing device, a metal casing in three-sided aluminium section, and two flanges which protect the screen fabric and contribute aesthetically to the product.

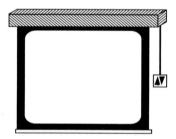

Fig. 8.1 Motorized projection screen

Measurement of the sound power level gives $L_{W_1} = 74$ dB(A) when this screen is operated electrically. (For the reader starting with this chapter, the levels L_W are usually higher than the pressure levels L_P, measured at varying distances from the appliance. Only levels L_W provide an objective quantity to compare different products, but only L_P levels give the users' sound comfort.)

If the metal casing is now removed (Fig. 8.2) the motorized screen is still perfectly usable, but loses much of its protection.

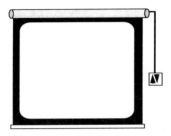

Fig. 8.2   The same screen, with casing removed

Operation of the screen now gives $L_{W_2} = 60$ dB(A). What does this 14 dB(A) difference represent? We have

$$L_{W_1} - L_{W_2} = 14 = 10 \log\left(\frac{W_1}{W_{ref}}\right) - 10 \log\left(\frac{W_2}{W_{ref}}\right)$$

$$10 \log\left(\frac{W_1}{W_2}\right) = 14 \qquad \log\left(\frac{W_1}{W_2}\right) = 1\cdot4 \qquad \frac{W_1}{W_2} = 25$$

With its protective and decorative casing the screen emits 25 times the power that it emits if used without it (Fig. 8.3).

This is, of course, the effect of the solid excitation of the casing structure by the motor, which is the vibration source. However, independently of any advantage of the latter, which of course will have consequences for the whole unit, these 14 dB(A) indicate potential improvements that could reward those willing to continue with us on this promising path.

The motorized unit installed

Figure 8.4 illustrates a typical arrangement of an installed motorized rollable screen.

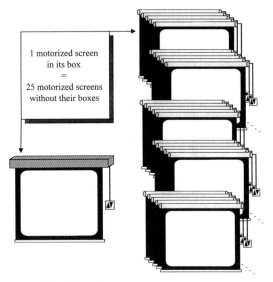

Fig. 8.3   A surprising comparison

First transmission medium: air

Independently of vibrations and noises generated by the equipment itself when in motion (for example, on a roller shutter the friction of the slats in the guiding rods), the noise and vibration source is the motor-gear ((1) in Fig. 8.4), which will give rise to so-called direct airborne transmission (even though this is across the rolling tube (4), the device still rolled up (6) and the casing (5)).

The rolling tube acts in principle as a screen to sound wave propagation, by obeying the mass law. The is true only for frequencies far away from the critical frequency. Furthermore, we must consider whether a long tube of this type lends itself particularly to propagation of waves coinciding with the tube's flexural modes.

In the closed cavity ((2) in Fig. 8.4) formed by the empty part of the rolling tube, stationary waves develop which excite its walls. The same happens in the cavity (3) between casing and

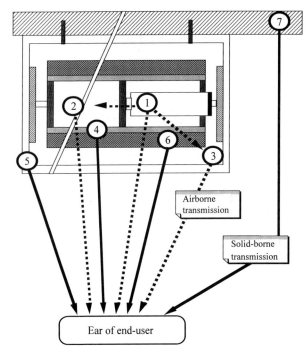

Fig. 8.4   Typical set-up and transmission paths

operational unit. The sound insulation afforded by the casing diminishes considerably if it has openings. A roller-shutter casing will give good insulation for a living room if it is hermetically sealed. The situation is typically much less favourable for venetian blinds and particularly, cinema screens.

Second transmission medium: solid structures
Solid-borne or structural transmission involves the conveying of vibrations directly by way of the different elements of the unit. Solid excitation of the rolling tube (4) and the functioning part (6) passes through the driving wheel and the bearing ring.

Solid excitation of the casing (5) occurs across the fixed point at one end and the end-cap at the other. Such excitation of the

167

ceiling or partitions (7) on which the device is mounted occurs across the casing attachments to the walls, or, depending on the situation, across the fixing braces.

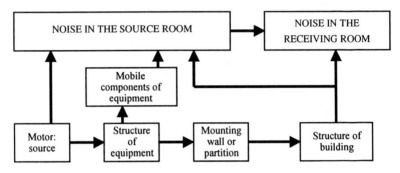

Fig. 8.5   The different transmission path

Figure 8.5 complements Fig. 8.4 in differentiating the source room (where the equipment is installed) and the receiving room. Most often it is the acoustic effects in the latter which need to be studied more attentively when installation conditions are being considered, which involve the architecture of the building. It is important to reduce to a strict minimum any disturbance towards neighbouring premises or housing: we are much more tolerant of noise we create ourselves than towards noise to which we are subjected.

Mix of approaches for combating noise

Is there then a miracle method to cut out completely the noise from the motorized building services plant in question?

Contrary to what happens for a finished product fresh from the factory—for example a vacuum cleaner or any other electrical domestic appliance—here there are several acting elements and it would be very tempting, for each one of them, to push this prickly question outside his field.

A motor with a gearbox designed without any noise-reducing features would inevitably produce vibrations, causing resonant modes in the lightweight structure on which it would be mounted.

On the other hand, a perfectly smooth and silent motor, designed, if money were no object, with precision-ground components, bearings on each shaft like a jewelled timepiece movement, would be very different.

Cost considerations justify the search for a compromise, combining all that is best in design, materials and installation practice.

Many years ago car manufacturers understood that it was possible to obtain—and did all they could to produce—an interior with high sound comfort level without expecting the combustion engine to become completely silent. Similar principles in the same field have been applied to the whole set of motorized equipment for electrical operation of windows, seats and so on. Such steps do not exclude a continual improvement of the motors used but certainly favour treatment of the systems as a whole.

As stressed in the Introduction and made clear by Fig. 8.5, effective effort against noise demands a global approach concerning

- the source, where component vibration should be minimized
- the end-product, where choice of materials and size of, in this case, rolling tube, fixing devices and casing are vitally important
- the installation conditions, by adapting the fitting accessories to the type of construction or, more effectively, by taking into account the criteria for motorization at the architectural design stage.

These are the subjects of the next three chapters.

9

Improvements at the source

Limits of reference

Manufacturers are unwilling to divulge confidential information collected in their test laboratories, even if it is out of date. This unwillingness is justified in today's competitive environment. But the purpose of this book is to promote progress and so a full description of the techniques used to reduce noise and vibrations in motors must be given. We have therefore made some (authorized) exceptions to the normal practice of industrial secrecy.

It goes without saying that, to different degrees and according to their means, all manufacturers act to improve their products' acoustic properties. The fact that a firm makes known its experience in this field can only advance its products' performance, to the great benefit of its customers. We have therefore taken as examples present or previous models of SOMFY motors, to highlight steps that have had lasting results. In some cases, relating to new products being developed, the results given bear on benefits obtained by the means adopted, rather than on absolute values not within the scope of this book and that can be found in the technical or commercial documentation which is easier to update. An improvement programme is always valuable: today's figures are better than yesterday's—and not as good as those of tomorrow.

Arrangement of a tubular motor

Figure 9.1 shows a tubular actuator, similar to the millions installed each year worldwide, semi-exploded to reveal its

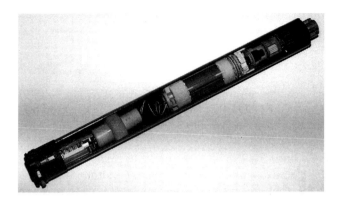

Fig. 9.1   Cut-away view of tubular motor

components. Consideration of its main parts will prepare the way for the inventory of causes of noise and vibrations given later in this chapter.

The motor
In most cases the motor itself is fed directly by an AC power supply (50 or 60 Hz depending on the country, between 100 and 240 V). It is therefore an asynchronous two-coil motor, called a single phase induction motor. The current in the second, auxiliary, coil, is kept out of phase with the current in the main coil by a capacitor, so producing a rotating magnetic field. In the most common arrangements (bipolar motors) this rotation matches the network frequency, 50 Hz or 3000 rev/min (or 60 Hz, 3600 rev/min) called the synchronization or supply frequency f_s.

If the motor is under no load, the revolving field pulls the rotor which then turns at a frequency f_r, very slightly lower than f_s. If the motor pulls an ascending load, the rotor rotation frequency decreases significantly. This lag between the frequencies of the rotor and the field is called the slip frequency.

The unitary slip S is the ratio of this difference in frequencies to the supply frequency. It is often expressed as a percentage

$$S = \frac{(f_s - f_r)}{f_s}$$

For low-power monophase tubular motors this slip at full load is typically 0·2–0·3 (20–30%), which means that, on a 50 Hz network, the full-load rotation frequency falls to 2400, even 2100 rpm.

These values for slip are much higher than those encountered on industrial three-phase asynchronous motors, where power is higher than 1 kW. Besides a scale effect, unfavourable for the output when size is reduced, this is explained by the special design of tubular motors which have to supply a very high torque, both when starting up and at normal speed.

If the motor is pulled by a descending load, it revolves at a frequency slightly higher than the synchronization frequency: it operates as an asynchronous generator. Table 9.1 gives an idea of the range of characteristics of different motors.

Table 9.1   Limit values for motor characteristics

Type	P_{mec}: W	Length: mm	Diameter: mm	Torque: Nm
min. 40	8·5	50	34	0·034
max. 40	14·3	80	34	0·057
min. 50	10·6	40	44	0·042
max. 50	69·1	100	44	0·275
min. 60	106	70	54	0·420
max. 60	186	115	54	0·740

Brake

It is essential that the motor is mechanically prevented from rotating when switched off, so it is not dragged by the weight of the load. This is achieved by a brake operating when there is no current, either alongside the motor (electric brake connected in parallel to the power supply) or incorporated into it (sliding brake which makes use of the motor flux).

Reduction gear
A reduction gear both lowers the rotational speed and raises the torque. To roll up a tube a speed of between 10 and 30 rpm is required, so that the reduction required is typically between 100 to 1 and 300 to 1. This is achieved by a three-stage epicyclic or planetary gear.

In each stage (Fig. 9.2) there is a central gear, the sun gear, encircled by two or more satellite gears which mesh simultaneously with the sun gear and the internally-toothed annulus or ring gear.

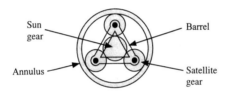

Fig. 9.2   Epicycloidal gear unit

The satellites are mounted on a barrel, which rotates if the annulus is fixed, conveying rotation, at reduced speed, to the sun gear of the next stage.

Normally the first-stage satellite gears are in injected polymer, those of the last stage in metal. The structure of such a gear unit gives a meshing frequency f_m equal to the output frequency multiplied by the number of teeth N_2 in the annulus. The reduction ratio is

$$1 / \left(1 + \frac{N_2}{N_1}\right)$$

where N_1 is the number of teeth in the sun gear. Table 9.2 gives typical values for the model of gear arrangement analysed for vibrations in the sections that follow.

Table 9.2   Frequencies associated with a gear

	Stage 1	Stage 2	Stage 3
Number of teeth: sun N1	9	7	7
Number of teeth: satellite	21	11	11
Number of teeth: annulus N2	51	29	29
Input frequency	f	$0.15\,f$	$0.029\,f$
Output frequency	$0.15\,f$	$0.029\,f$	$0.006\,f$
Meshing frequency	$7.65\,f$	$0.846\,f$	$0.164\,f$

Counter

About a quarter of the volume of the actuator is taken up by a counter which, once set, allows the motor to be switched off when the moving element reaches either its upper or its lower position. It does this by counting the number of revolutions made by the tube on which the element is rolled. Indirectly, this tube rests on an outer annulus on the motor. This component acts as a bearing whose revolutions are counted in either direction.

The tube

The whole unit is fixed on a frame inside a metal tube, typically 1.5 mm thick; the length and external diameter vary depending on the power range

- length 423 mm in range '40'
- length between 386 and 566 mm in range '50'
- length between 550 and 663 mm in range '60'.

Table 9.3 shows the characteristics of a complete tubular motor.

Connections

The dephasing capacitor is placed inside the tube, between the revolution counter and the motor. The wiring between motor,

Table 9.3   Complete motor units: characteristics at 50 Hz

Type	Pelec: W	Length: mm	Diameter: mm	Speed: rpm	Torque: Nm
ARIES	75	423	37	14	4
ARIANE	90	386	47	16	6
VECTRAN	290	566	47	12	45
TITAN	420	550	57	12	100

revolution counter and supply cable is also passed through this space.

Causes of vibrations and noise

Motor-induced vibrations

The motor can generate vibrations either by strictly mechanical or electromagnetic effects or both. The first electromagnetic effect results from the elliptical nature of the rotating field. Because the currents supplying the coils are not accurately shifted in phase by 90° and do not necessarily have the same amplitude, the revolving field is not constant throughout the rotation and describes an ellipse (Fig. 9.3). This makes the force acting on the rotor vary and produces torque pulses on the motor shaft with frequency f_1, double that of the field (two maxima per revolution)

$$f_1 = 2f_s$$

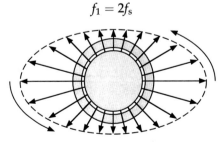

Fig. 9.3   Rotating elliptical field

The second electromagnetic effect is magnetostriction. To avoid propagation of high currents, induced by variations in the magnetic flux in the mass of steel of the rotor and stator, it is essential to make them of metal sheets or laminations. These are metal plates insulated electrically from each other by surface treatment to increase the resistance of the metal parts. However, in the presence of an external magnetic field, all the laminations behave as one magnet and attract each other, to cause compression of the stack whenever the field is strong and whatever its direction. Here then is a new source of vibration of frequency f_2 in the stator, with

$$f_2 = 2f_s$$

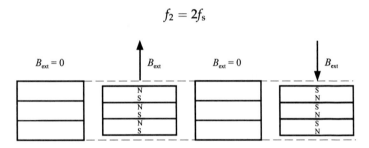

Fig. 9.4 Magnetostriction

The third electromagnetic effect is caused by the slots. There must be enough space in the soft-steel structure, which has to guide the magnetic flux, to house the copper conductors which create the flux (stator) and the aluminium ones which, in the rotor, allow circulation of the induced currents that start the rotation. These conductors are therefore placed in the spaces, in other words the slots.

The presence of notches introduces an angular dissymmetry in the circulation of the magnetic flux between stator and rotor which leads to a reluctant torque. The teeth tend to attract each other and it is when they coincide that the maximum flux— sought by any magnetic structure—is achieved. In relation to an imposed rotation, a motor torque occurs when the teeth

Fig. 9.5   Reluctant torque at the slots

approach each other and a really reluctant torque when the teeth are apart (Fig. 9.5).

For the same number of notches N_e on the rotor and stator the pulsation frequency f_3 is this time related to the rotation frequency f_r

$$f_3 = N_e f_r$$

But that is not all. These periodic changes in the configuration of the magnetic circuit also lead to variations in the amplitude of the revolving magnetic field, which reinforce the preceding pulsations.

Added to these torque pulses is another, similar effect, but this time in the plane of the laminations, perpendicular to the axis. Under the influence of the mutual attraction of the teeth, the laminations periodically tend to stretch radially. These radial constraints, which can be large, balance each other if there is an even number of teeth (Fig. 9.6).

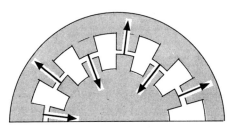

Fig. 9.6   Radial stresses

Fig. 9.7   Example of lamination profiles used

To counter all these effects, it is normal practice to use different numbers of teeth for stator and rotor, as illustrated in Fig. 9.7.

Otherwise, use is made of the rotor's laminated structure to set each lamination at a slight angle from the preceding one to form inclined slots by skewing the rotor slots by half the stator slot pitch.[15] One therefore obtains a spatial averaging favourable for all the phenomena produced by the notches. But nothing is gained without special care. Fig. 9.8, for example, shows that the

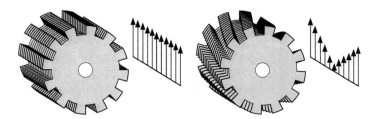

Fig. 9.8   Rotors with straight slots (laminations aligned, left) and inclined (laminations skewed, right)

notch inclination can generate a differential moment on the shaft, which could induce in the bearings a vibration level higher than the one that this solution is supposed to overcome.

Of course—and this does not simplify matters—all the foregoing phenomena and those that follow, occur simultaneously. At work here therefore are combinations of the frequencies mentioned (sums and differences) and their harmonics because the pulsations produced are far from being sinusoidal.

Now for the more commonly known, purely mechanical causes of vibrations (Fig. 9.9). These are found in any rotating system.

- First mechanical cause: static unbalance. This results from a displacement of the centre of gravity in relation to the axis of rotation.
- Second mechanical cause: dynamic unbalance. This occurs when the principal axis of inertia does not coincide with the axis of rotation.
- Third mechanical cause: bending of the shaft. Slight bending gives rise to in-phase axial and radial pulls on the bearings.
- Fourth mechanical cause: pitching of the shaft. External forces this time induce axial and radial pulls in phase opposition on each bearing.

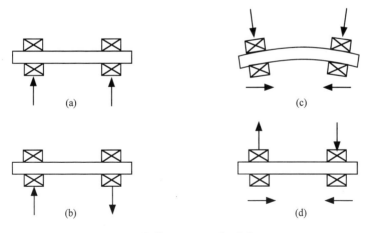

Fig. 9.9   Different types of unbalance

In most cases the vibrations generated by these mechanical defects have the rotation frequency (few harmonics)

$$f_5 = f_r$$

Bearings

A motor axis may be carried by sleeve bearings or rolling bearings and sometimes a different type at each end.

A bearing of mean diameter D comprises an internal ring, an external ring and n balls of diameter d. With a hypothetical non-slipping ball bearing, a defect on an internal ring or an external ring will generate vibrations of frequency f_6 or f_7

$$f_6 = \frac{n}{2} f_r \left(1 - \frac{d}{D}\right) \text{ and } f_7 = \frac{n}{2} f_r \left(1 + \frac{d}{D}\right)$$

Experimental results and interpretation

Framework of the study

The GEMINI 25/16 motor served as a reference in the study conducted by the Vibration and Sound Laboratory of the INSA in Lyon.[16] The motor tube was 496 mm long with an external diameter of 47 mm. The complete motor had mass 2·4 kg and could pull a load with a resistance torque of 25 mN (70 kg on a 70 mm diameter pulley) at 16 rpm. The stator had 12 slots, the rotor 17. Two bearings were used on the motor

- one on the gear side: 8 balls; $d = 3·5$ mm; $D_{ext} = 17$ mm; $D_{int} = 10$ mm.
- the other on the free side: 7 balls; $d = 3$ mm; $D_{ext} = 15·4$ mm; $D_{int} = 9·4$ mm.

Vibration analysis

The behaviour of the motor on its own followed distinct lines fitting almost perfectly the phenomena described in the given list, in which the numerical values for the motor itself and its rotation frequency (in the 50 Hz mains) are shown.

Table 9.4 Frequencies produced by the gear unit

Frequencies: Hz	No load		Lowering 70 kg		Lifting 70 kg	
	Calculated	Measured	Calculated	Measured	Calculated	Measured
Shaft rotation	49	49	52	52	39	38
Bearing 1— external ring	146	146	153	144	114	—
Bearing 2— external ring	130	126	137	132	102	—
Bearing 1— internal ring	248	242	261	260	194	188
Bearing 1— internal ring	214	212	225	—	168	162
Stator slots	591	588	621	—	462	—
Rotor slots— fundamental	837	834	880	878	654	652
Rotor slots— harmonic 2	1674	1664	1760	1756	1308	1304
Iron sheets vibration	100	100	100	100	100	100

Table 9.4 gives the frequencies calculated, or measured on this spectrum, or in complementary tests (not represented) with nominal load in the two rotation directions.

When the motor is linked to a gear, a spectacular increase in background noise is observed: 10–20 dB across the range, and nearly 30 dB at low frequencies. The gear therefore contributes significantly to the overall vibration power.

In Fig. 9.10, the cursor of the spectrometer is positioned on a line at 373 Hz which does not appear in the spectrum for the motor on its own. It is a first-stage meshing frequency. A broader spectral analysis (0–3·2 kHz) (not shown), can pick out the energy peaks to identify the set of spectral lines, as shown in Table 9.5.

There is almost complete agreement between theoretical and measured values. Particularly noteworthy is the fact that the

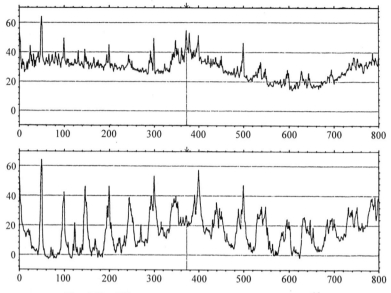

Fig. 9.10   Vibratory spectra under no-load conditions[16]

lines associated with the rotation frequency change position depending on whether there is no load, a pulling or pulled load. One important result is that the vibration spectrum (0–3·2 kHz) also produces a strong decrease in the average vibration level when the frequency increases.

Acoustic analysis
The vibration analysis just dealt with is complemented by analyses of overall sound pressure (with spectral distribution), and of intensity.

In the intensimetric analysis twelve measuring points were distributed evenly on a generating line 10 cm from the motor axis. Two other points were taken on the axis, each side of the two ends. The intensity measured on the axis is more than 3 dB less than that measured at right angles to the tube: the emission is therefore essentially radial, coming predictably from the

Table 9.5   Ranges of sound pressure levels

Frequencies: Hz	No load		Lowering 70 kg		Lifting 70 kg	
	Calculated	Measured	Calculated	Measured	Calculated	Measured
Meshing 1st stage	376	373	396	396	295	294
Lateral bands	328/426	426/422	344/448	344/448	256/333	258/—
Harmonic 2	752	754	792	792	589	588
Lateral bands	704/803	—	740/844	740/842	550/628	552/628
Harmonic 3	1130	1134	1188	1188	884	886
Lateral bands	1081/1180	1084/1184	1136/1239	1138/1238	845/923	844/920
Harmonic 4	—	—	1584	1584	1178	1180
Lateral bands	—	—	1532/1636	1534/—	1140/1217	1140/1220
Meshing 2nd stage	42	42	44	44	33	—
Harmonic 2	83	82	88	88	65	64
Harmonic 3	125	126	132	132	98	98
Harmonic 4	167	168	176	176	132	132

motor and gear, with an average level also 3 dB higher than that measured at right angles to the part housing the connections and revolution-counter. In the spectral distribution, both for pressure and intensity, there is an overwhelming predominance of high frequencies.

Comparison of spectra—radiation factor
For simplification, the frequency field is divided into three zones according to the octaves included

- low-frequency (LF), with the 125 and 250 Hz octaves
- middle-frequency (MF), with the 500 and 1000 Hz octaves
- high-frequency (HF), with the 2000 and 5000 Hz octaves.

Figure 9.11 gives a comparison of the contributions of each zone to the overall level. It shows that the vibration spectrum at low

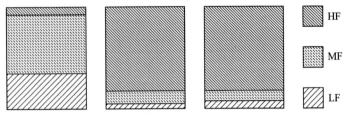

Fig. 9.11   Vibratory spectrum (left), L$_P$ spectrum (centre), intensity spectrum (right)

frequencies is quite strong (left), whereas less strength is apparent in the sound pressure (centre) or intensity (right) spectra.

The radiation factor of the motor tube explains how HF vibrations which are a minority in the vibratory mode resolutely take over in the sound mode. The radiation factor σ expresses the relation between the sound power radiated and the vibratory power brought into play (Appendix 4). It is in effect the yield of the conversion of energy, mechanical waves and sound waves.

$$\sigma = \frac{(\text{Emitted sound power})}{(\text{Vibratory power})}$$

The sound power is determined from intensimetric measurements, as seen in Chapter 8. The vibratory power is calculated from the mean square velocity, measured using an accelerometer. It is thus possible to determine the radiation factor.

In the case studied, an overall radiation factor of less than 5% (0·046) is obtained. However, Fig. 9.12 shows how inconstant is the tube's radiation factor. It is this capacity of the tube's structure to change vibratory energy into sound energy at high frequencies that explains the spectral distributions obtained by the complete motor.

Conclusions
Without pretending to be exhaustive, this account has shown that the causes of vibrations and sound emissions are clearly

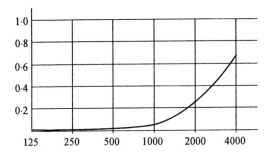

Fig. 9.12   Radiation factor of motor tube[16]

identified for the main frequencies. But the extreme complexity of the spectrum of secondary lines, which contribute greatly to the overall level, does not facilitate improvements.

The presence of well-marked vibration frequencies is a potential cause of excitation of the structures linked up to the motor. The number of these frequencies, the fact that they are well spread out (except at high frequencies) and their position which generally varies with the velocity, and therefore with the load, makes it impossible to avoid provoking some of the structure's resonant modes. In the first place it is the amplitude of these excitation frequencies that must be reduced.

The presence in the spectrum of pure high-level frequencies inevitably produces stationary wave effects in semi-anechoic spaces, which distort the noise measurements. Similarly, source directivity phenomena are no longer negligible for these frequencies if the latter are high. Therefore to determine accurately the sound properties of tubular motors a reverberation room is needed, or intensimetric measurements.

Preliminary improvement of the motor

Type of modifications
The results just described demonstrate how important are the gears, particularly of the first stage, in producing vibrations. The

185

only measures that can be applied, short of a complete redesign of the product, incorporating the acoustic aspects in a more general framework, can only involve improvements compatible with the existing structure, such as optimization of the size and shape of the teeth, but keeping the overall geometry of each part.

Special efforts are made to reduce manufacturing tolerances of the basic components. Divergences resulting from super-imposition of tolerances explain why, in the same manufactured batch of a type of motor, some are noisier than others.

The planetary gears are made of injected polymer (polyamide for example) and several nominally identical copies can be produced simultaneously from multiple impressions in the same mould. Component variability stems from dimensional differences between the impressions, temperature and pressure gradients in the mould, external conditions and physico-chemical properties of the material. The components manufac-tured for SOMFY reach the highest possible performance levels in injection technology.

The tests

All the comparative tests described in this section have been conducted as determinations of pressure L_P, according to the standard in force at SOMFY up to 1994: measurements in a semi-anechoic room, at 1300 mm from the motor axis and 1350 mm from the floor, by a BK 2209 microphone and BK 2143 analyser. The spectral analysis is achieved by averaging over linear time for 10 s, breaking down into one-third octave bands and correction by A-weighting.

Measurements are taken during a rising cycle, a descending cycle, and unloaded. In the latter case, the motor is simply suspended from the building support by cords or luggage elastic. In the measurements under load the motor pulls a heavy pulley, fixed to the solid building structure by a device that prevents transmission of vibrations to it. It is the motor alone that is to be tested.

In order to validate the results obtained from the above modifications (applied from January 1993), 50 motors of the 30/16 model were taken by sampling from one batch of the series, before introducing the modification. They were all tested using the procedure indicated, their gear was replaced by another manufactured according to the new process, then retested.

The results

Table 9.6 first gives an idea of the spread of the results. It shows the maximum divergence between the levels of the noisiest and quietest motors of the batch.

Table 9.6   Ranges of sound pressure levels

Divergence: dB(A)	No load		Up		Down	
	max	σ	max	σ	max	σ
Before modification	11	2·2	6	1·5	5	1·6
After modification	9	1·8	6	1·3	5	1·3

The standard deviation σ is a statistical quantity representative of the way in which the population tested is grouped around the mean. The results are distributed noticeably according to a 'normal law': 68% of the samples are within the range $\pm\ \sigma$ and 95% within $\pm\ 2\sigma$ of the mean value.

The first effect of the modifications therefore is to limit scatter of the results, notably by reducing the value of the mean divergence. The modified motors are more uniform in their sound characteristics.

However, the results on the average overall sound level, in Table 9.7, are even more significant. Remember that actuators used to be much noisier in lowering than in lifting operation.

Table 9.7   Improvement of measured sound levels L_P (dB(A))

	No load	Up	Down
Gain: dB(A)	7	2	7

Modifications produce an equal level in both cases. The sound level when there is no load has also been improved, to 7 dB. There is still a difference of 14 dB between the sound level with no load and that under full load. The sound spectra in Figs 9.13–9.15 give the comparative results for one-third octave bands between 50 Hz and 20 kHz. The value given in each band is the arithmetic mean of the levels of 50 samples.

The spectrum when there is no load (Fig. 9.13) brings out the strong contribution from the 100 Hz vibrations which diminishes significantly after modification. This may surprise some people because the motor itself has not been altered. The 100 Hz vibrations are produced by the laminations and the torque pulses resulting from the elliptical field.

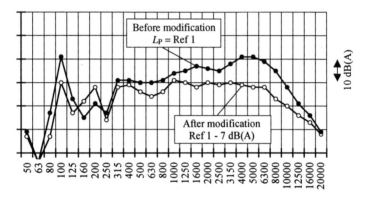

Fig. 9.13   Average spectrum for motor without load

An optimum shape and dimensions of the gear teeth prevents these torque pulses from causing microshocks on the teeth. In other words, the motor has not been improved here, but the gear has become much more tolerant of its pulsations. The gear proper is more subdued at medium and high frequencies, which just shows the first stage's role in noise generation.

On the spectrum for the lifting operation in Fig. 9.14 the pressure level is much higher than when the load is zero. The purely electromagnetic effects are insignificant compared with

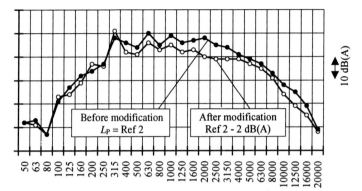

Fig. 9.14 Average spectrum for motor with pulled load

vibratory components induced by the gearing. The predominance of the meshing frequency and its harmonics is expressed
by a high contribution of the 315 and 630 Hz bands. Only a slight
improvement is achieved by modifying the gear. This improvement, is however, very marked for the descent (Fig. 9.15). To the
ear, the disappearance of the peak of the 1600 Hz is very
noticeable, in the same way that fluctuations of noise with time
tend to become blurred: the regularity of the sound level makes
it more pleasant.

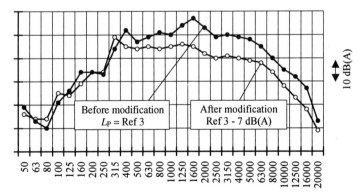

Fig. 9.15 Average spectrum for motor with pulling load

Another improvement approach

Type of modifications
Here we deal with more extensive modifications bearing on the structure of the product, allowed by a complete renewal of the range.

Figure 9.16, the first example, is a cut-away view of a gear of this new generation. The reason for the changes is a combination of considerations of resistance of materials to fatigue or wear, distribution of constraints, ease of assembly, but always with the objective of improving the acoustic or vibratory performance of the whole unit. Not only the meshing components but also the support plates have been redesigned.

The dimensions of the motor itself have been arrived at by taking into account the results mentioned previously, which contribute markedly to the behaviour of the whole.

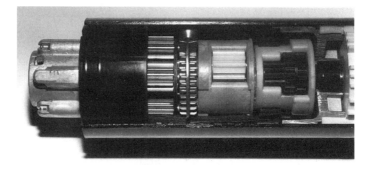

Fig. 9.16   New SOMFY gear from LT range

The tests
The results given here come from batches of motors, for the approval of new products. They concern LT50 motors made completely with components from production equipment.

According to references, the batches comprise between 15 and 60 motors.

Between this new generation and the previous one, SOMFY changed from a standard of measurements in a semi-anechoic chamber to tests in a reverberation room which allow the sound power of products to be measured. These comparisons are, of course, conducted with motors from the old range (already improved as described previously), placed under the new measurement conditions, and deal with the gain in sound pressure level. The batches of the old range LS50 comprise between 5 and 15 motors.

The results

Table 9.8 gives, for each of these tests, the gain obtained on the average level, with no load, with a pulled load and a pulling load and the gain obtained on the standard deviation.

With one exception (and for operation without load), highly significant gains have been obtained. This does not appear in the table, but the deviation between the lifting function and the lowering function is also narrow. In this way up to 1·9 dB(A) is gained in addition to those already obtained in 1993.

However, the disparity of the gains illustrate how difficult is the struggle against noise. Even if, from one model to another, the same principles are applied, the results may be different.

Table 9.8   Improvements in terms of sound levels L_P obtained for LT range (dB(A))

Type: torque/speed		6/17	10/17	15/17	20/17	25/17	40/12
No load	Average gain	2·0	2·5	4·1	7·0	1·6	−1·7
	Gain in σ	−0·1	0·6	0·0	−0·6	−0·1	−0·2
Up	Average gain	3·6	5·1	8·7	8·4	4·5	2·4
	Gain in σ	0·3	0·6	0·0	−1·1	0·0	0·0
Down	Average gain	3·3	6·8	9·8	10·4	2·4	4·8
	Gain in σ	0·1	0·2	−0·5	−1·4	0·1	0·3
Number of samples: LT/LS		39/15	31/15	15/10	40/10	59/10	35/5

The table indicates that substantial gains on sound pressure level can be accompanied by degradation of the standard deviation. This is the case for example of the motor 20/17 when lifting, which gains 8·4 dB(A) on average but loses 1·1 in standard divergence. Overall, there is definite progress since 95% of this type of product will gain between 10·6 dB(A) at best, 6·2 dB(A) at worst.

A continuing process

. . . but limited

The results presented here show what improvements can be obtained. However, it would be optimistic to assume that the same type of action, repeated every six months, would always yield gains of the same value. It has to be admitted that some of the lines of approach explored produce disappointing, or even negative results, without any of the causes becoming evident.

The improvement process is nevertheless a continuous one in the design offices and new features are incorporated in the manufacture whenever tooling is renewed provided that concrete gains have been confirmed. However, each triumph over the effects of one spectral line accentuates a neighbouring one, ignored until then, which then becomes the target for further intensive improvement efforts.

Durability: compare like with like

One can well imagine, however, that in this type of campaign the most significant benefits are achieved early on. Once established, there is less room for manoeuvre and necessary compromises have to be made. For instance, some materials can reduce noise but to the detriment of motor durability. It would be wise not to sacrifice durability on the altar of the fight against noise. Nevertheless both considerations must be scrupulously taken into account in comparisons of materials, particularly when they come from different sources.

Speed: use the same conditions for comparisons

As far as motorized equipment is concerned, we must not forget that the rated speed is another key factor in comparative tests. For the same load a slower motor is necessarily less noisy, because it transmits a lower mechanical power. It is not a minor phenomenon. Far from it: any type of transmission causes a growth in noise of around 6 dB(A) for every doubling of rotation frequency, for a given load.[16]

A little puzzle: between one motor Y, for sound power L_W of 60 dB(A) with full load and at 15 rpm, and another make X producing 58 dB(A) at 10 rpm under the same load, the quietest is not the one we might have thought . . . In fact, objectively motor Y is the quieter: by 1 dB(A), when the comparison is brought down to identical terms. If it were capable of pulling the load at 15 rpm (i.e. a 50% increase in speed), motor X would radiate a sound power

$$L_W = 58 + \left(\frac{6}{2}\right) = 61 \ (dB(A))$$

10

Improvement of the moving unit

CSTB testing methods

In the context of the research entrusted to the Grenoble Sound Laboratory of the CSTB, the objective is to improve the completed unit, without modifying the motor, which is taken as it stands. Improvements affecting the overall product design should be clearly distinguishable from those obtained by changes to the source.

All the units fitted with SOMFY motors have the same basic structure, the motorized axis (Fig. 10.1), consisting of

- the actuator itself (not altered at all this time)
- the rolling tube
- the driving wheel and the crown wheel
- the end-cap.

The tube is held at one side by the end-cap and at the other by the annulus/revolution counter assembly, which acts as a bearing.

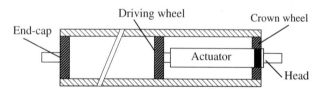

Fig. 10.1   Motorized tube

The dimensions of the different elements depend on the application, but the structure remains the same. Casings and fastenings are much more varied and specific to each type of product. The investigation was therefore divided into two parts, with the following steps.

- On the basic product, the motorized tube
  - analyse the conditions, make observations
  - interpret findings, look for the propagation paths
  - make improvements
  - . . . and finish off the series of steps if necessary.
- On the specific types of equipment, representing each main family (roller shutter, venetian blind, or projection/cinema screen)
  - quantify the possible benefits
  - look for the reasons for an improvement or deterioration
  - improve the product, when the design allows for this to be done simply
  - formulate recommendations.

The CSTB has a large-volume reverberation chamber (75 m^3), where standard sound power measurements can be performed on different appliances (according to the standard NF S 31022 *Determination of sound power emitted by noise sources*).

The measurements are conducted by one-third octave bands from 50 to 5000 Hz, using the following equipment

- a microphone BK 4166, mounted on a portable stand, with an AKSUD 11C supply
- a digital tape recorder – TEAC RD 200T
- a chart recorder – BK 2306
- a BK 2143 analyser, linked to a personal computer by IEEE bus.

Acceleration measurements, which lead to the determination of the vibratory energy, are performed using accelerometers – BK 4374, with supply from BK 2635.

The basic unit: the motorized tube

The motor chosen is a 30/16 (nominal torque 30 Nm, nominal rotation frequency 16 rpm), arranged in a tube of 60 mm diameter and 1·50 m in length. The actuator, in 1 mm thick steel, occupies a third of this length. All the tests with the motorized tube are performed without load: the motor pulls only the tube and nothing else.

For convenience, in this type of test, it is preferable to suspend the tube from a bracket using baggage elastic. When the motor is switched on it rotates inside the tube which does not move, a perfectly normal situation from the point of view of acoustics.

The findings
Figure 10.2 gives a comparison between the motor alone and the motorized tube, of the power levels and spectral distribution. The result is an overall deterioration of around 3 dB(A) when the motor is placed in the tube, with resonances particularly in the 160, 800 and 1600 Hz bands. All the power levels measured between 125 and 1000 Hz are at least 10 dB(A) higher than those caused by the motor alone.

Beyond 2000 Hz, however, the levels become inverted. The tube then acts as a better phonic screen than one could have

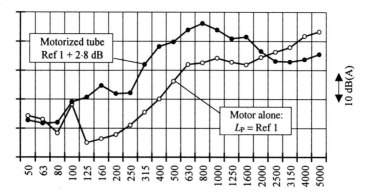

Fig. 10.2   Sound power of actuator alone and motorized tube

wished to see in the whole spectrum. From 2000 to 5000 Hz, the mass law fits quite well: combined with the increase in the source power level (about 6 dB per octave), noted in this interval for the motor alone, the decrease of 6 dB/octave resulting from the mass law leads to a markedly constant level.

Elsewhere in the spectrum the resonances completely mask the tube's role as screen, a role which in any case is smaller the lower the frequency.

Interpretation

The resonances observed can come from several sources

Sound: longitudinal stationary waves. In the air in the free part of the tube longitudinal stationary waves form, whose frequencies for different modes (*i*) is given by

$$f_i = \frac{ic}{(2L)}$$

Taking the free part of the tube (1 m) as L and 340 m/s for the velocity c of sound in air, the first three modes appear at 170, 340 and 510 Hz. This effect can explain in particular the peak observed in the 160 Hz band.

Sound: transverse stationary waves. Taking radial waves this time, tube length L is replaced by its diameter D (0·06 m) in the above equation. The first two modes appear at 2833·and 5666 Hz, frequencies that do not stand out on the spectrum, which excludes any significant effect of this type of excitation.

Vibrations: solid excitation. Transmitted by the driving wheel and the crown wheel, vibrations excite the tube as transverse ones. The mode frequencies can be calculated by considering the tube as a slender beam supported at its ends. Taking the properties of steel (density, Young's modulus), for the first four modes one obtains 171, 683, 1537 and 2733 Hz (Appendix 4). These values are indicative since they depend on limiting conditions, but emphasize the tube's ability to react by resonance in the range of the frequency considered.

197

Similarly, excitation by a ring mode is possible, but the corresponding frequency would be 27 kHz.

Vibrations: flexural waves from bending of the tube by excitation of the surrounding air. Waves are generated when sound waves impinge on the wall of the tube. For 1 mm steel, the frequency is 10 kHz and therefore is not applicable.

Treatments

Significant information on the relative importance of resonance or propagation modes can be gathered by way of efficient sound or vibration treatments (Fig. 10.3).

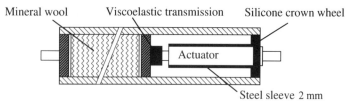

Fig. 10.3   Combined treatments

Treatment for *airborne effects* consists of the following.

- Reduction of the direct emission from the motor, by inserting it in a steel sleeve 2 mm thick. Treatment by confining the motor is highly sensitive to sound leaks (see Chapter 4 in the section on Non-uniform walls). In order to control these, the motor tube surface at the gear end is covered with an insulating mastic. The area corresponding to the annulus and the fixed point is not treated.
- Reduction of the level of stationary waves inside the free part of the tube, by filling it with an absorbent material (mineral wool or fibreglass).

Treatment of *solid-transmitted effects* consists of insulating against vibration between motor and tube by the following methods.

- The insertion of a viscoelastic coupling. This is a product from the PAULSTRATM catalogue, Miniflex model, whose size here is appropriate for a small load (5 Nm). Taking into account the torsional stiffness of the rubber used and the dimensions of the coupling, the theoretical resonance frequency is 7 Hz.
- Replacement of the plastic wheel of the revolution-counter by a moulded foam silicone ring.

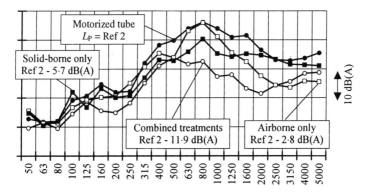

Motorized tube
L_P = Ref 2

Solid-borne only
Ref 2 - 5·7 dB(A)

Combined treatments
Ref 2 - 11·9 dB(A)

Airborne only
Ref 2 - 2·8 dB(A)

10 dB(A)

50 63 80 100 125 160 200 250 315 400 500 630 800 1000 1250 1600 2000 2500 3150 4000 5000

Fig. 10.4   Compared effectiveness of different treatments against sound power

Results

- Treatment of *airborne effects* alone: this produces an overall damping of about 3 dB(A). It is completely ineffective at the frequency for the maximum sound emission (800 Hz), which shows that the latter is in the solid-borne transmission domain. Above 800 Hz, this treatment proves to be highly effective. The gain is around 6 to 10 dB depending on the frequency band.
- Treatment of the *solid-borne transmission* only: the overall damping this time is nearly 6 dB. Solid transmission is twice as great as airborne transmission. The beneficial effect of solid insulation begins to be noticeable from 200 Hz.

● Combined treatment of *airborne* and *solid-borne trans-mission*: the overall damping this time is about 12 dB(A). Notably the resultant gain is greater than the sum of the gains obtained previously, as Fig. 10.5 indicates. Combination of the two treatments mathe-matically should give 53 dB(A) for the remaining L_P, whereas the real figure obtained is only 49·3 dB(A). At first surprising, this is a result of the *interaction of treatments,* as follows.

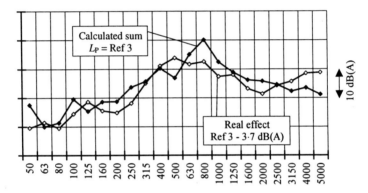

Fig. 10.5   Sum of the effects and effects of the sum

○ Interaction of treatment for sound on solid-borne transmission: this effect stems from the insertion of the insulating sleeve, stiffening the motor tube, which serves as a reference for aligning motor components. The result is a reduced vibration level of the motor itself.

○ Interaction of the treatment for vibrations on airborne transmission: the source of sound waves generated inside the tube is mainly the motor, but the pulling wheel also contributes. The vibration insulation of this reduces the level of stationary waves in the tube . . . and of the interaction between source and medium.

○ The sound and vibratory power emitted by the motor is not independent of the propagation medium, which is not at all like free-field conditions.

Motorized tube: conclusions
All these interactions result in the fact that there is no one specific feature that can be targeted to produce a miracle cure. Instead, combination of the whole set of treatments is required to obtain significant improvements. Unfortunately this is not the most comfortable situation for the designer, who must spread his anti-noise 'budget' thinly to gain maximum benefit.

Substantial improvements will also result from good choice of rolling tube, which must as far as possible limit the amplitude of bending or torsion waves: thickness, stiffness, circular rather than polygonal section.

PVC window-shutter unit

Window-shutter unit
As in all sectors, there is a tendency in the building industry to prefabricate a set of elements that combine to fulfil the same function. The combination window-shutter, or window-shutter unit (Fig. 10.6), available in either PVC or aluminium, thus offers an attractive alternative to the series of operations, installing a window frame, then a roller shutter casing and then the shutter itself. These components are all incorporated in the window-shutter unit, delivered ready to install and preset for such functions as the path of the motorized roller-shutter.

Installation
The window-shutter unit is installed in the reverberation room, placed on a flexible seal and fixed to the wall by two braces bound to the window frame and insulated from the wall by antivibration pins. A plaster casing BA 13 is fixed around the

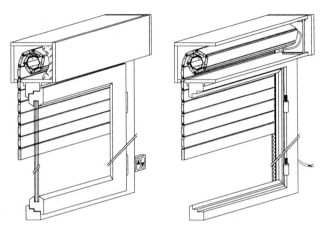

Fig. 10.6   Window-shutter unit

window. Inside this casing the wall is lined with glass fibre to eliminate reflections and therefore simulate a free field.

Parallel to the wall of the room, a Placostil™ partition is built around the window, to a height of 2·5 m and width of 4·6 m. The experimental installation is shown in Fig. 10.7. The window-

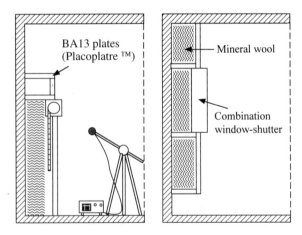

Fig. 10.7   Installation of the window-shutter unit in the reverberation room

shutter unit can thus be tested, it being assumed that the sound power radiated in the reverberation chamber is the same as that of a functioning unit fitted permanently in a building. The shutter is 1 m wide and is pulled by a 25/16 actuator.

Findings
The first three tests are conducted without load, to assess the motor, the axial motor and the efficiency of the casing (Fig. 10.8). The sound power of the motor alone, with no load, serves as reference level.

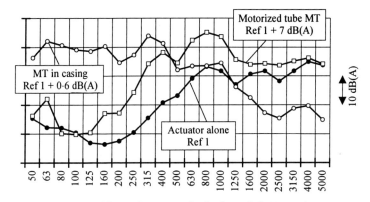

Fig. 10.8 Motor alone, motorized tube and shutter casing

When the driving wheel, the annulus, the tube and the end-cap are added, the level increases to 7·2 dB(A), which corresponds to a fivefold increase in emitted sound power. The inherent defects of the axial motor structure, seen previously, appear once again. The tube shape, hexagonal and perforated in this case, is not very resistant to deformations.

However, the insertion of the motor tube in the casing causes the sound power level to fall by 6·6 dB(A). This advantage indicates the good design of the PVC casing

●   the motorized tube is fixed laterally using PVC flanges running along the side of the casing: these flanges have a much stronger damping effect than a metal attachment would have

• the walls of the PVC casing produce hardly any resonance.

Low frequencies do, however, excite the casing walls. Owing to the A-weighting, the overall level is hardly affected.

The four subsequent tests, under load, confirm that the PVC structure behaves well, in the face of solid-transmitted excitations. Again the lowering operation is noisier than the raising manoeuvre (+2 dB(A)). Spectral analysis reveals the high-amplitude low-frequency components induced by the slats sliding in the runners.

When the cover is removed from the front of the casing, there is a large power increase (10–12 dB(A)). If the transmission was of the solid-borne type, the opposite would happen. The casing then acts perfectly as a screen and does not cause any amplification. Table 10.1 summarizes these findings.

Table 10.1 PVC window-shutter unit: difference in sound power level L_W (dB(A)) compared with motor without load

1	Actuator 25/16 without load: reference level	0
2	As above + driving wheel + crown + tube	7·2
3	As above, inserted in closed PVC casing	0·6
4	With load—UP—casing closed	1·7
5	With load—UP—casing front removed	14
6	With load—DOWN—casing closed	3·3
7	With load—DOWN—casing front removed	13·9
8	With load—UP—casing closed, motor in 2 mm thick steel sleeve	−3

Vibration speed determinations are performed by placing an accelerometer at different points of the structure. They confirm that the transmission towards the glazing and the uprights is very weak. The sound energy emerges mainly from the casing, by airborne transmission (Fig. 10.9).

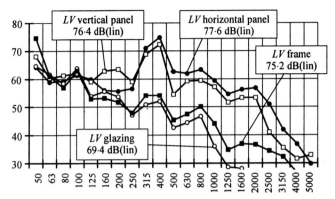

Fig. 10.9   Vibration spectrum (LV = mean square velocity level) of the PVC window-shutter unit

Treatment

Under these conditions, the recommended treatment (if necessary, since the power levels are satisfactory here) will be of the airborne effects. The sound treatment effected in the case of the motorized shaft (addition of a sleeve round the motor, packing with glass fibre) is enough to improve the level, which falls by 5 dB(A) in comparison with the corresponding test (No. 4).

It is not certain that a treatment of solid-borne transmission by using a viscoelastic connection between the motor and the roller could reduce the level emitted even further. Because of the elasticity of the attachment flanges of the roller, there is a great risk of forming a double mass-spring system, as described in the section on Degrees of freedom of the suspended structure in Chapter 7. Addition of elasticity to an already elastic system does not improve it. It may even degrade the behaviour.

Aluminium window-shutter unit

Unit tested

The component used is a French window with one door, 200 cm high under the casing and 133 cm wide. The casing side is 20 cm.

The glazing itself is 100 cm wide. The rolling tube has a small diameter (40 mm), which leads to the choice of an LS 40 8/14 (8 Nm, 14 rpm).

Installation
The unit is installed in the same way as before, such that the sound power radiated towards the interior of a space can be determined in real time. A type of plasterboard is fixed around it: height 240, width 100 and 110 cm on each side, giving a partition of total surface area 5.3 m^2.

Findings
As in the above section, the first three tests aim to assess the motor alone, then the motorized axis by itself, then fitted in the closed casing, to gauge the efficiency of the latter. Fig. 10.10 shows the spectra obtained.

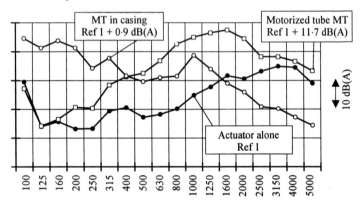

Fig. 10.10   Motor alone, motorized tube and shutter casing

The sound power under load is determined by the series of tests set out in Table 10.2. As in the previous case insertion of the motor in the rolling tube causes a large increase in the sound power level, by nearly 12 dB(A). However, the casing again is a good insulator, as it gives a damping effect of 11 dB(A). The

Table 10.2   Aluminium window-shutter unit: difference in sound power level L_W (dB(A)) compared with motor without load

1	Actuator 8/14 without load: reference level	0
2	As above + driving wheel + crown wheel + tube	+11·7
3	As above, inserted in closed aluminium casing	+0·9
4	With load—UP—casing closed	+2·7
5	With load—UP—casing front removed	+12·2
6	With load—DOWN—casing closed	−1·9
7	With load—DOWN—casing front removed	+6·9

motor used behaves in the opposite way to the previous one, producing a much lower vibration level under pulling load (lowering) (or with no load) than with pulled load (lifting).

Vibration speed measurements show how, as in the previous case, the casing is predominant in sound emission. At the resonance peaks, the difference in levels between time mean square velocity of the casing and the time mean square velocities of the frame or the glazing is greater than 10 dB (lin). The vibration level of the casing is however much lower

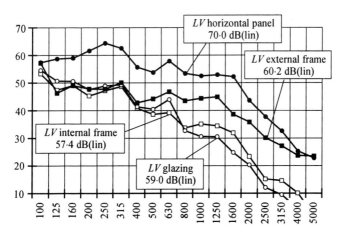

Fig. 10.11   Vibration spectrum of aluminium window-shutter unit

here than for the PVC unit (an improvement of 12 dB (lin). The reasons are explained further on.

Treatments

This is another example of a manufactured building element, optimized acoustically in spite of a serious handicap compared with its PVC counterpart, which has a much higher vibration damping coefficient by internal loss on bending.

The casing proves to be highly effective, even though in metal, and the structure as a whole suffers little excitation. This stems from the manufacturer's meticulous design. The whole of the internal walls of the casing is lined with a thin (3 mm) flexible-sheet sound insulator (FSI, see the section on General rules in Chapter 12) which is enough to prevent resonance in the metal sheets, contributes to aerial insulation and adds heat insulation. Also, an elastomer seal is inserted between the casing and the metal frame of the window. Solid transmission is really reduced to a minimum. This is an example of a product designed to eliminate all noise from manual or motorized operation.

When using such products, it is at the installation stage where substantial improvements can be obtained, as shall be seen in Chapter 11 in the section on Installation of window units.

Venetian blind

The construction of the motorized venetian blind is shown in Fig. 10.12. The same motor serves to keep the slats in the correct orientation and to raise and lower the blind. This is done by a tilter which carries a cylindrical element through an almost complete turn between two stops. Having turned in one direction or the other and arrived at a stop, this cylinder slides on the rotation axis if the latter continues to turn. Two or more thin cord ladders are joined to the rocker, whereas two narrow bands, the lifting cords, roll up round the tube.

Although its structure is particular, the venetian blind used

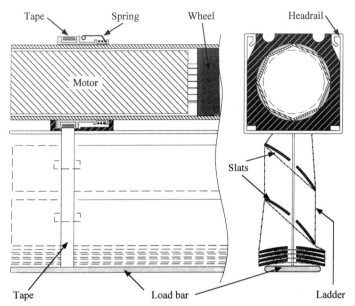

Fig. 10.12   Venetian blind drive system

has all the elements of a motorized tube: motor, ring, drive wheel and tube, octagonal in this case. The motorized tube is, however, not suspended from the fixed point on the motor and a bracket, but with special plastic fittings that act as bearings, attached in the tube.

The blind is 1 m long. For the tests in the reverberation chamber, it is fixed on the PVC window casing by standard fixing plates.

Findings
Three tests were first conducted, with no load, to assess the motor, the motorized tube and the efficiency of the casing. The sound power level emitted by the motor on its own is taken as reference.

When the fittings and the octagonal tube are added the level rises to about 2 dB(A). However, when the motorized tube is

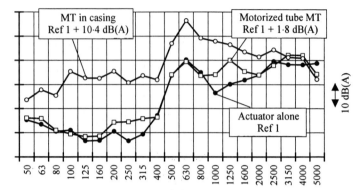

Fig. 10.13   Sound power spectra for venetian blind

placed in a U-shaped casing, and operates without load, the emitted power level grows by 8·6 dB(A). This casing has a disastrous effect because it favours several resonance modes.

Two tests are conducted under normal operating conditions, on raising and lowering of the complete unit. The results are almost identical and show little difference from the behaviour when there is no load, when the pulling straps were severed. An interior venetian blind motor does not carry much load compared with its nominal torque and slides very little.

Treatments
The results indicate that a better design could reveal a potential gain of 10–12 dB(A). The improvement is bigger the more the dimensions of the blind favour resonance phenomena in the casing. A second, 2·65 m long, venetian blind complete with driving mechanism, mounted on a solid wall, was provided with damping treatment (viscoelastic bitumen) of the metal, a cover over the top and viscoelastic suspension for the motor. The results (Fig. 10.14) speak for themselves: a 19 dB(A) gain.

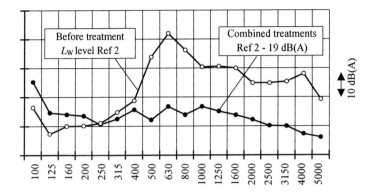

Fig. 10.14   *Sound power level L$_W$ for venetian blind, 2·65 m, before and after modifications*[18]

Projection screen

Structure

The screen studied is 2 m long × 2 m high. It rolls up on a 1 mm thick steel tube of 50 mm diameter, and is driven by a 6 Nm/16 rpm. Inside it is like a motorized tube fitted to an aluminium casing. This casing consists of an L-shaped mounting structure and a facing plate held by screws. The motorized tube is attached to the aluminium profile by two end braces.

Findings

Tests were performed under loaded conditions, for both ascending and descending operations.

In the first test, the complete screen was used normally. Sound power level was 75·1 dB(A) on ascent, 73·6 dB(A) on descent. During the time for a complete ascent (about 30 s), the average level decreases by about 3 dB, whereas on descending it increases by about 6 dB. This phenomenon comes from the unrolling and rolling of the screen fabric around the tube. The fabric acts here as a sound insulator.

In the second test the facing plate of the casing is removed.

The power level during the ascent diminishes, to 72·6 dB(A), and the same happens on the descent, to 70·0 dB(A).

In the third test, the casing is removed completely. The screen is still operational as a motorized tube. There is a large drop in emitted sound power: to 61·8 dB(A) on ascent, 60·2 dB(A) on descent.

Treatment

This model of screen has undergone a rigorous detailed investigation, conducted by SOMFY's German subsidiary.[17]

For convenience, measurements have been made of sound pressure level L_P, at a distance of 1·35 m and height of 1·38 m.

Table 10.3 *Combined effect of improvements on projection screen*

	Gain: dB(A)	T1	T2	T3	T4	T5	T6	T7	T8	T9
M1	0									
M2	4	✔								
M3	2		✔							
M4	1			✔						
M5	6	✔		✔						
M6	4	✔		✔	✔					
M7	11	✔		✔		✔				
M8	5			✔		✔				
M9	6			✔		✔	✔			
M10	10	✔		✔		✔	✔			
M11	4			✔				✔		
M12	9	✔		✔				✔		
M13	9			✔				✔	✔	
M14	9			✔				✔	✔	✔
M15	4			✔				✔		✔
M16	9	✔		✔				✔		✔

The summarized results (Table 10.3) are a guide rather than absolute values. The treatments are

- T1: mounting on vibration isolators added to supporting flanges
- T2: attachment of flanges to the frame by rubber rings
- T3: rubber drive wheel (stiffness too great)
- T4: loose joint between facing plate and frame
- T5: damping bands stuck on at different points ($\Delta M = +2\%$)
- T6: rubber ring on revolution-counter annulus
- T7: flocking of polypropylene fibres ($\Delta M = +1\%$)
- T8: bearings in Hytrel^{TM}
- T9: tube filled with plastic foam.

By far the most effective treatment consists of coating the casing plates with a viscoelastic material to absorb vibrations. These treatments combined with fitting of a suspension on the motor lead to improvements of 10–17 dB(A).

11

Improvement of installation conditions

Products and installation conditions

The motorized products described in the previous chapter include only a small sample of the many automatic closure and solar protection devices used in buildings. The projection screen and the venetian blind are representative enough of interior products for studying the influence of installation conditions, but the same cannot be said for prefabricated integrated elements such as the window-shutter unit, which leave little room for variation and represent only a small part of the range of exterior products available.

Concerning roller shutters, attention should be brought to the so-called traditional products, single-unit elements and those installed in tunnel-casings. For exterior blinds, the representative cases of the swivel-arm and projecting type are taken as examples.

Traditional roller shutter
The traditional roller shutter is a set of wooden, PVC or aluminium slats, attached by straps to the roller tube of the motorized tube, which is usually fixed to the masonry by metal braces. It rolls up inside a casing which can be fixed partly inside the building (traditional interior type) or completely on the outside (the traditional exterior type). Figs 11.1 and 11.2 show how such elements are installed on the building.

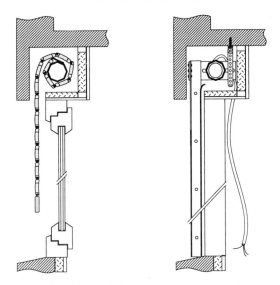

Fig. 11.1   Wall integrated roller shutter (traditional, internal)

Renovation roller shutter module

Monobloc (French term) modules are also called renovation shutters because most often they are fitted to replace others, or as protection that was not originally envisaged when the building was constructed. (Warning: in Germany, monoblock means a combination window-shutter.)

The motorized tube is this time fixed on the flanges of a metal casing, which rests directly on the runners. The latter are fixed to the masonry on the outside, as shown in Fig. 11.3.

Roller shutter in tunnel casing (or lintel roller shutter)

The tunnel casing is a neat means of incorporating the roller shutter into the building structure. It is a hollow lintel element, made of fibralite or expanded polystyrene for example, over which concrete is poured when the building shell is constructed. The motorized shaft is fixed on the flanges which are inserted into the masonry.

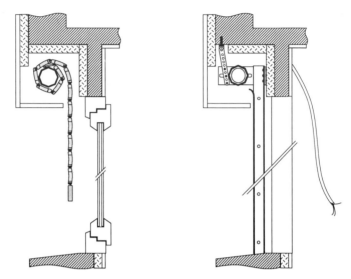

Fig. 11.2   *Wall integrated roller shutter (traditional, external)*

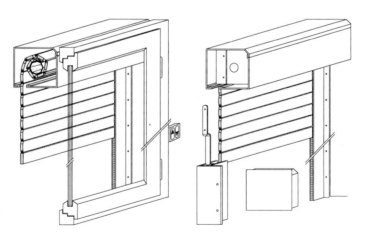

Fig. 11.3   *Renovation roller shutter module*

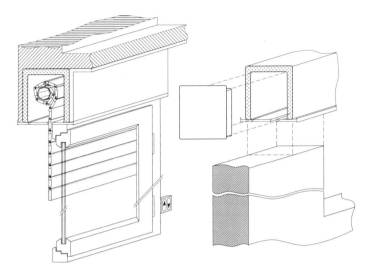

Fig. 11.4   Roller shutter in lintel casing

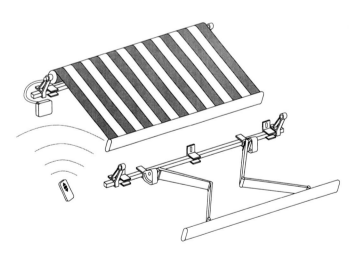

Fig. 11.5   Folding-arm awning

Folding-arm awning

A folding-arm awning in principle rests on a hollow square metal bar, arranged horizontally, at each end of which are held the fixtures of the motorized tube (Fig. 11.5). This bar is mounted on the façade by two braces. It also holds the anchorage points of the two articulated arms (arm, elbow and forearm) at the end of which a front bar is attached.

The blind fabric is attached at one end to the front bar and at the other to the roller. Two strong springs set in the elbow joints press against the front bar, which thus keeps the fabric taut. This kind of blind is found typically on individual private houses or small commercial premises (protection of shop windows, café terraces and so on).

A cassette awning has the same structure but is integrated with a casing which protects the whole of the blind when rolled up and closed. The movable bar at the end of the fabric often serves as the casing cover. This is constructed of metal and must be carefully designed to prevent resonance.

Pivot-arm awning

Pivot-arm awnings are more common in collective housing or tertiary sector buildings. The motorized axis is fixed to the

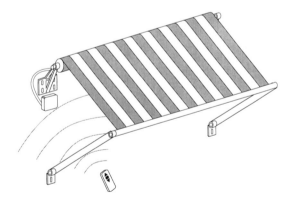

Fig. 11.6 Pivot-arm awning

masonry by braces. The fabric is kept taut simply by the weight of the bar framework (Fig. 11.6).

Construction of the building
Conditions and methods for installation of interior products, window-shutter units and the abovementioned elements depend greatly on the type of construction and more especially on

- whether the walls are light or heavy
- the heat insulation: whether it is internal or external.

There are a great many variations in each category of wall. In traditional construction of both collective or individual housing, most often in Europe there is a system of horizontal slabs and supporting walls poured on site.

The façade (16 cm thick traditionally) is then either poured on site simultaneously, or filled out, afterwards with hollow breeze-block or brick masonry, which gives a façade of either large (concrete) or medium mass (breeze-blocks or bricks). However, light façades are also encountered, for which the filling serves mainly as thermal insulation. Laminated wood with polystyrene, fibre glass or mineral wool is used.

In tertiary buildings façade elements are often placed on a metal support (aluminium), to cover the whole surface of a window unit and form a curtain wall.

Thermal insulation fitted inside is important in damping solid-transmitted vibrations, whereas externally placed insulation will have hardly any influence.

Automatic control
In addition to all the parameters that must be considered related to sound transmission, there are systems whereby an individual or group of elements (by master control) can be operated automatically, as illustrated in Figs 11.7 and 11.8.

Choice of field test sites

The list of products cited is restrictive, but there are already seven of them. These can be installed in three types of building (individual, collective, tertiary), on two types of wall (heavy or light), with two possible means of thermal insulation and two kinds of potential use.

Suppose that we wish to enumerate all these parameters: a provisional total of combinations will be $7 \times 3 \times 2 \times 2 \times 2 = 168$, without going into the detail of the subject! Variations possible for each configuration have been ignored, otherwise the number of combinations would grow exponentially.

It is common, while waiting for a programme of industrial and scientific research to commence, to find ways of significantly reducing the number of tests applicable to the multiple combinations of independent factors that act on a given process. Evidence shows that this method would unfortunately not have

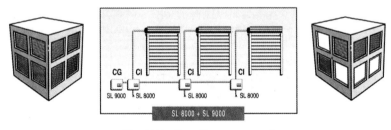

Fig. 11.7   Overall group control

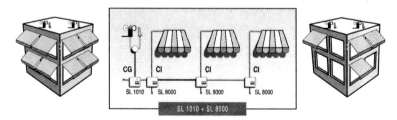

Fig. 11.8   Automated wind or solar protection system

much impact in this case. We prefer to leave this course to future generations and adopt a more intuitive approach, whose logic will appear to the reader through the numerous conclusions to which it leads.

Six test sites only have therefore been selected. This small number masks a much greater number of combinations. We have endeavoured to choose these sites so that a large number of products and modes of operation can be tested simultaneously in one type of building. Table 11.1 summarizes the combinations covered by the different sites.

The window-shutter units are not featured in this necessarily limited experimental study, but the measurements taken in the context of product improvement, described in Chapter 10, give sufficient information on which to base several recommendations, which are gathered in the section on Installation of window units in this chapter and that on Specific products in Chapter 12.

Table 11.1 Combinations of conditions covered by field tests

	Building use			Wall		Insulation		Control	
	Indiv.	Collect.	Tertiary	Light	Heavy	Int.	Ext.	Indiv.	Group
Interior: venetian blind	—	—	FT1	FT1	FT1	—	—	FT1	FT1
Interior: screen	—	—	FT1	FT1	FT1	—	—	—	—
Roller shutter traditional interior	FT2	—	—	FT2	FT2	FT2	—	FT2	—
Roller shutter traditional exterior	FT2	FT3	—	—	FT3	—	FT3	FT3	FT3
Roller shutter tunnel casing	FT4	—	—	—	FT4	FT4	—	FT4	FT4
Folding-arm awning	FT5	—	—	—	FT5	FT5	—	FT5	—
Pivot-arm awning	—	FT6	FT6	FT6	FT6	FT6	—	FT6	FT6

Owing to SOMFY's industrial division's location, the sites are all situated in the French department of Haute-Savoie. Some have led to simple observations whereas others have resulted in a true evaluation of work done to improve installation methods and conditions. We will now review the tests in more detail.

Field test FT1

Description of site
The first field test gives the properties of the interior products: venetian blinds and film projection screen. These are installed in a conference room in a tertiary building of traditional construction. The room is rectangular (9 m × 7 m), with height to the ceiling of 3 m, and gives on to a largely glass façade on one side and a corridor on the other (Fig. 11.9).

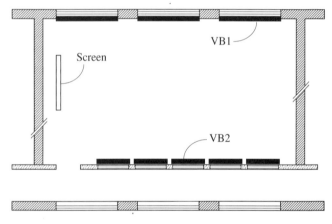

Fig. 11.9   Room plan showing surrounding spaces

The façade is in 30 cm thick concrete. The windows are fitted with interior venetian blinds (VB1). Two supporting walls, also in concrete, separate the room from adjacent ones. Between the room and the corridor is a glass partition on a wooden structure. Other venetian blinds (VB2) can cut off the room visually from the corridor. Carpeting covers the floor, and an acoustic false ceiling is suspended 30 cm from a concrete slab ceiling. A projection screen is fitted into this false ceiling.

Venetian blind VB1
The blind tested, VB1, one of many attached to the façade, is 2·65 m long. It is fixed directly to a concrete lintel. Solid transmission of vibrations occurs on the heavy wall but the vibration velocity levels are insignificant. As there are no thermal insulation panels or lightweight structures supported by the inside of the façade, these solid vibrations have no acoustic effect. The study therefore starts with a situation where the installation conditions in no way affect adversely the sound characteristics of the product tested.

This does not mean that the product does not deserve our attention. A particularly pronounced resonance from the casing makes it excessively noisy and justifies the corrective treatment already described in Chapter 10 under the heading Venetian blind. We will not return to this, except to to recall that it brings an improvement of 19 dB(A).

Venetian blind VB2
Figure 11.10 shows the detailed construction of the venetian blinds fitted in the partition separating the room from the corridor. Here the situation is unfavourable for such an installation, since the product this time is mounted on a light structure.

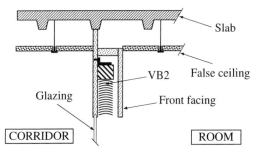

Fig. 11.10   Mounting of a venetian blind VB2 on glazed partition

The venetian blind tested is 1·20 m long. It is assumed that no change will be made to the product itself, but rather to its installation environment.

The construction includes a wooden concealment hood and the first modification consists of cladding the interior face of this with rock wool. Fig. 11.11 shows that this straightforward measure brings an improvement of 8 dB(A) in the sound power level. However, this level is still much too high because of the decision not to eliminate the strong resonance occurring in the metal casing.

The next step is to fix the product on the same part of the partition, but using viscoelastic suspension units. This results in almost no improvement in the conference room itself. The measured sound power level comes essentially from airborne transmission radiating from the product as a whole. The high value of this explains why the lateral facing is so effective when it is treated appropriately. This does not mean that the suspension has no effect. Fig. 11.12 shows the vibration speed of the partition glass, before and after fitting the suspension. Measurements are performed with an accelerometer, as described in Chapter 8.

Analysis of the power transmitted by the partition shows that the component radiated by the glazing is predominant. From

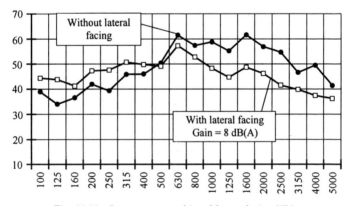

Fig. 11.11   Improvement achieved by enclosing VB2

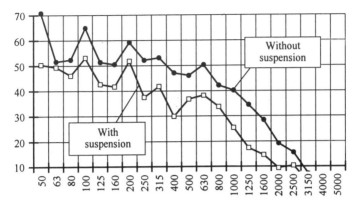

Fig. 11.12   Vibration: mean square velocity LV of glazed partition (dB (lin))

known data on the radiation coefficient of the equivalent of 5 mm glazing, the total power radiated towards the corridor is calculated to decrease from 49 to 39 dB(A).[18]

In the case of VB2 an improvement of 8 dB is achieved over the interior level by using a lateral facing, whereas use of a viscoelastic suspension for fixing the product causes a 10 dB(A) reduction in the sound power radiated by the partition to the adjacent spaces.

Projection screen

The film projection screen is inserted in the aluminium casing, itself fixed to the concrete ceiling by four stiff rods. The false ceiling rests on the bottom of the lateral faces. A 10 cm layer of rock wool is laid on the false ceiling and is wrapped over the screen (Fig. 11.13), which is therefore quite well insulated for airborne transmission, at least for three faces and two side pieces or flanges.

Removal of the false ceiling could therefore be expected to increase the sound power level transmitted to the room. Fig. 11.14 shows the result: the sound insulation effect of the false ceiling is zero. There is even an improvement of 0–2 dB(A) in the frequency bands higher than 2 kHz when the false ceiling has

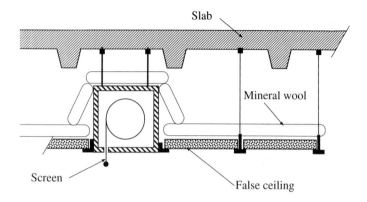

Fig. 11.13   Arrangement of film projection screen

been removed. This can be explained quite simply. The panels of the false ceiling, rest on the sidewalls of the screen and are thus subjected directly to the solid excitation of the casing. They radiate at least as much power as they absorb from elsewhere (aided by the rock wool) to contribute to the airborne transmission. Just a small adjustment is needed to cure this effect and re-establish the false ceiling's sole function as insulation (see Fig. 13.6).

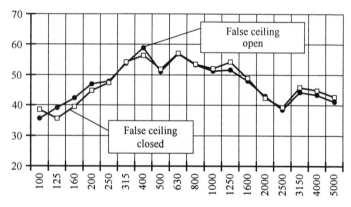

Fig. 11.14   Influence of false ceiling

Field test FT2

Description of site

The field test 2 set-up makes it possible to assess the noise produced during operation of motorized roller shutters, mounted traditionally either internally or externally. It consists of an installation in a one-storey house, with exterior and supporting walls in concrete and interior walls in brick. Fig. 11.15 is a simplified plan of the situation. The roller shutters are an old wooden-slatted model. The metal runners do not carry either a brush or rubber damper. Considerable noise is produced by knocking and rubbing between the slats or between the slats and the runners.

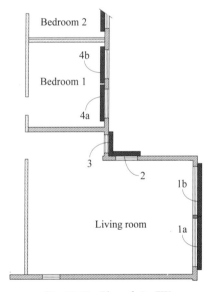

Fig. 11.15   Plan of site FT2

Installation in external casings

The first observation concerns shutters for the living room, all fixed in external casings. Measurements for this and the following sites are conducted for standardized pressure levels, values brought back to the standard reverberation of 0·5 s.

Figure 11.16 compares pressure spectra during operation of shutters 1b and 2 measured in the living room. There is a large

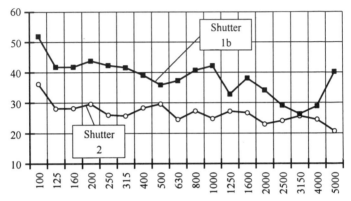

Fig. 11.16 Pressure level L_P spectra (living room) on operation of living room shutters

difference of 12 dB(A) between the two, which cannot be explained by the difference in size of the two types of shutter. Shutter 1b is three times as large as shutter 2: the sound power it produces could be taken as three times as great, which would give a difference of 5 dB(A) in level, not 12 dB(A).

The mounting methods in fact explain the considerable difference. The cause is not to be found in the two casings, which are identical in construction, but in the solid transmission through the runners. In shutter 2 this solid transmission has no effect, as the runners are attached to the concrete framework posts. The runners for shutter 1b (and 1a), however, are screwed directly on to the timberwork of the window unit and induce solid-transmitted excitation in it.

Installation in internal casings
In bedroom 1, the shutters are fixed in the traditional way in an internal plywood casing. The sound level in this room is high.

The shutter runners are arranged correctly, but this time the fixing brackets for the motorized tube have been screwed into the upper part of the timber window casement instead of being fixed into the concrete. By attaching the anchorage points to the concrete, the sound level can be improved by 8 dB(A) (Fig. 11.17).

The pressure level received in the adjacent rooms stays around 35 dB(A), both in bedroom 2 when shutter 4b is operated and in the living room when shutter 4a is operated. It is carried by solid-borne transmission, noticeably identical before and after changing the motorized tube fixture point.

Only a viscoelastic suspension added to the tube would reduce the level of sound transmitted, as we will see in greater detail in field test FT3.

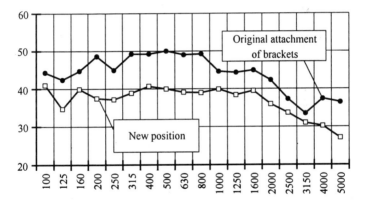

Fig. 11.17   Pressure level L$_P$ spectra (bedroom 1) on operation of shutter 4a

Field test FT3

Description of site
The situation this time is a small two-storey block of six flats. The outer facing is in hollow 20 cm breeze-blocks in its turn

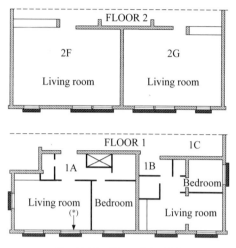

Fig. 11.18   Plan of site FT3

covered externally by a layer of polyurethane then by a timber boarding. In this building we concentrate on sound transmission between adjacent flats through its structure. This type of transmission implicates the supporting walls which are also 20 cm breeze-blocks. Partitions are in hollow brickwork. The slab between the two storeys is a flooring in small girders and pugging 20 cm thick with an under-level crossed by heating pipes, mounted on polystyrene supports and covered by a coating and tiling (Fig. 11.19).

Effects of suspension of motorized tube in the source room
It must first be noted that installation of roller shutters in traditional external casings leads to excellent results for sound control. Before any corrective treatment, operation of the shutter tested in the living room of flat A generated a sound pressure level of 35 dB(A). A basic viscoelastic suspension was therefore attached to the motorized tube (Fig. 11.20). This reduced shutter-operation noise in the source room (living room 1A) by 4 dB(A) (Fig. 11.21).

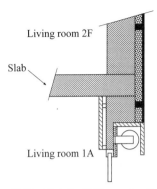

Living room 2F

Slab

Living room 1A

Fig. 11.19   Detail of FT3 construction

Although thermal insulation for this building is largely on the outside, the main rooms are clad with wooden panelling which can be affected by vibrations of the solid structure. In such a situation a suspension device, added primarily to reduce transmission to the adjacent rooms, also improves conditions in the source room.

Fig. 11.20   Experimental viscoelastic suspension (courtesy of SOMFY)

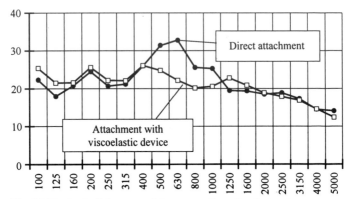

Fig. 11.21 L_P in living room 1A on operation of a shutter in same room

Vertical solid-borne transmission
The fitting-out of flat 2F in the block, situated on the floor above the previous one (1A), had not been finished at the time of the field test and the lining of wooden panelling was not yet in place. There was therefore no light structure to be set in vibration by solid-borne transmission along the vertical solid wall when the shutter of living room 1A was operated. Addition of a suspension to the motorized tube of this shutter gave a smaller improvement in the receiving room (living room 2F) than in the source room (Fig. 11.22).

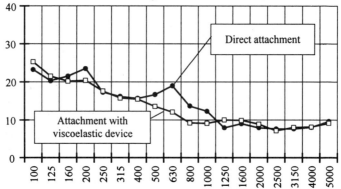

Fig. 11.22 L_P in living room 2F on operation of shutter in living room 1A

The sound levels transmitted were, moreover, weak and could be measured here only because of particularly favourable circumstances: heavy snowfalls had strongly reduced the background noise (20·8 dB(A)). The levels measured indeed approached background values in some frequency bands, which helped to mask the improvement.

Contrary to what could be expected, the wooden panelling in flat 2F, once fitted will, for the case without suspension, probably give a lower sound level than the bare walls. Rest assured that even in the worst case the resultant level will remain lower than the threshold 30 dB(A).

However, addition of a suspension to shutter 1A when the panelling is in place brings a more substantial improvement. In living room 1A suspension reduces only the solid component, whereas a significant proportion of the shutter operation noise comes from airborne transmission through the glazing. There is therefore only a partial improvement, albeit 4 dB(A). There is all the more reason for the reduction to be much greater, because transmission between 1A and 2F is almost entirely of the solid type. The vibratory speed measured on the façade of 2F, when shutter 1A is operated, indicates the potential gain that can be

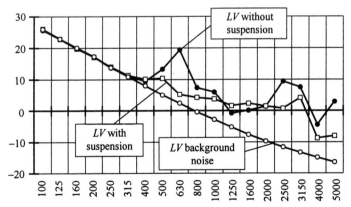

Fig. 11.23 *Mean square velocity level (LV) measured on wall of living room 2F*

achieved by fitting a suspension. In the most prominent frequency band the improvement is about 15 dB(A)!

Horizontal solid-borne transmission
The effects of horizontal transmission are much less marked than those of vertical transmission, from one floor to the next above, owing to a greater distance travelled and consequent greater damping influence of the structure. For example, operation of an unmodified shutter, in bedroom 1A (Fig. 11.18) induces sound levels of 37·5 dB(A) in that room and of 27 dB(A) in living room 1B. Conversely, simultaneous operation of all three, unaltered shutters in flat 1B gives only 26·3 dB(A) in flat 1A bedroom.

Field test FT4

Description of site
The use of tunnel (lintel) casings for roller shutters is encountered particularly in individual houses. This is the case of the installation at site FT4, for which we limit ourselves to straightforward observations and interpretations (Fig. 11.24).

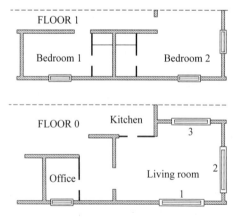

Fig. 11.24 Plan of site FT4

The construction is recent, with a high-quality finish and concrete floor slab. The walls have an internal thermal insulation skin, with a compound of plaster and polystyrene. The shutters are in aluminium, with insulated slats.

Sound levels measured in the source rooms
Shutters are fitted in the office and in the living room. In the office, much too high a sound level, 58 dB(A), was detected. This resulted from a fault typical of the installation. In fact, the shutter was fitted on a French window and the motor used had a secondary switching mechanism operated by a winding handle. Attachment of this handle system required perforation of the casing (probably larger than necessary) which has not been treated for noise. Airborne transmission is therefore high, which explains the high level measured, for a shutter of otherwise average dimensions. In the living room, the window units are practically double the size of the one in the office, and the sound levels are much more bearable: 36–38 dB(A).

Solid-borne transmission
For the same shutters, the acoustic pressure levels have been measured in the rooms on the floor above. Figs 11.25 and 11.26 show how much these rooms are affected. In some frequency bands the level is higher in the receiving room (bedroom 2) than in the emission room (living room).

Again the result was seen of solid excitation in the façades, transmitted to the lightweight insulation panels inside and, in this case, mainly of excitation of the slab. Addition of suspensions could effectively solve the problem, so long as the casing flanges are suitable (see Chapter 12 under the heading Specific products).

The same strong effect was found in the case of bedroom 1 above the office, with a sound level of 41 dB(A) when shutter 1 is operated. In the case of simultaneous operation of the lower-floor shutters, a high sound level of 42 dB(A) is found in bedroom 2 when closed up.

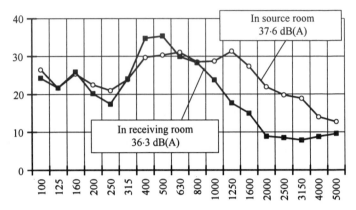

Fig. 11.25   L$_P$ of living room (source room) and bedroom 2 (receiving room) on operation of living room shutter 2

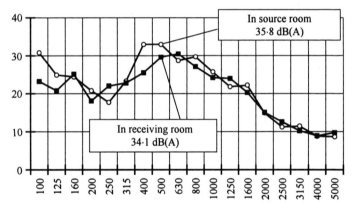

Fig. 11.26   L$_P$ in living room and bedroom 2 on operation of living room shutter 3

Field test FT5

Description of site

The site for FT5 was used to assess the installation conditions of an exterior folding-arm blind or awning, fitted to the front of an individual house of façade 100 m², consisting of a ground floor and an upper floor with bedrooms.

The façade was constructed in hollow concrete breeze-blocks 20 cm thick. Thermal insulation was internally arranged (with a plaster and polystyrene composite). The slab between the two floors was in 20 cm reinforced concrete. On the façade itself, reinforced concrete panelling was used instead of hollow breeze-blocks. The blind was fixed to the façade by two brackets, embedded in the concrete panelling, below the level of the slab (Fig. 11.27).

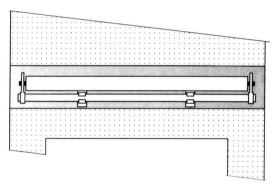

Fig. 11.27   Blind attachment to building FT5

Findings

When the blind was operated, the sound pressure level measured in the first-floor bedroom was exceedingly high, around 37 dB(A), easily explained by a considerable amount of solid-borne transmission. To improve on this, viscoelastic suspension was added, attached as in FT3. Fig. 11.28 gives a comparison of the sound pressure levels before and after putting the motor tube under suspension. They changed from 36·9 to 36·3 dB—an insignificant improvement! But as in any field, some failures in the combat against noise are generally beneficial and give food for thought.

In the case studied, the brackets were placed about 30 cm from the supporting bar, whereas the fixing nuts of the motor

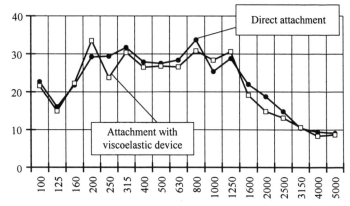

Fig. 11.28   Effect of attaching axial suspension

tube were at each end of the tube. There is therefore some elasticity between the fixing point of the viscoelastic suspension and the rigid point.

Here we have arrived at the formidable situation described in the section on Degrees of freedom of the suspended system in Chapter 7, where it was shown that we cannot argue against the laws of physics. Fortunately the answer is simple: just by bringing the fixture points closer to the suspension points, good results are achieved (Fig. 11.29).

Field test FT6

Description of site
We shall finish the chapter with a similar field test on façade awnings mounted on two very different types of tertiary building: of heavy and lightweight construction (Fig. 11.30).

The heavy structure is made up of prefabricated reinforced concrete modules, in which each window unit has a metal framework supporting double glazing. This light frame rests on the concrete structure, held by a mastic sealant. The blind is arranged in a concrete housing which protects it from the

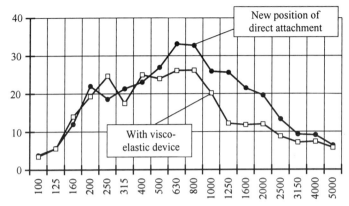

Fig. 11.29   Effect of attaching brackets conforming to principles

elements. The motorized tube is fitted directly into the concrete structure. The communication bridge between the buildings in Fig. 11.30 is typical of a lightweight tertiary construction, entirely

Fig. 11.30   Situation of façade awnings studied (courtesy of SOMFY)

239

in metal and sheet glass. The floor, 32 × 2·5 m in surface area, is carpeted. A false ceiling, with no noise reduction features, hides piping and ducting. Blinds are fixed to the structure with highly rigid brackets. One motor operates two or three blinds and the intermediate brackets serve only to hold up the transverse bearings.

The objective of the measurements conducted was to confirm that the structure determines the sound level, while showing what improvements are possible in unfavourable situations.

Arrangement on a heavy structure: individual and group control
Once again, the advantages of such an arrangement are confirmed and quantified. In an office the standardized measured sound pressure level produced by operating a blind is 31 dB(A) for a background noise of 27 dB(A).

For an overall control of the whole group of blinds on the façade, this level rises by only 1–2 dB(A), even though 14 motors are activated simultaneously and the chosen office is situated in the middle of the façade.

Remote operation of the whole set of blinds, except those in the receiving room, gives a sound pressure level inseparable from the backgound noise.

Arrangement on lightweight structure: individual and group control
It would not be surprising to find a very high level in the lightweight structures. Fig. 11.31 gives the results when individual control is used, before and after improvement, which is achieved in two stages

- replacement of an LS motor by the new LT model (giving an improvement of 6·6 dB(A));
- addition of a viscoelastic suspension on the fixed end of the motor, the sleeve bearings and the end-cap (improvement of 3·4 dB(A)).

The improvement perceived subjectively is much higher than the raw figures would suggest. This is true for the whole set of

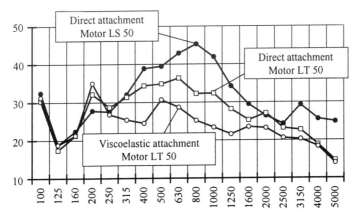

Fig. 11.31   Blinds on communication bridge FT6 (courtesy of SOMFY)

changes using a viscoelastic suspension fixture. This effect results from the spectral composition of the noise, whose high frequencies, which are always unpleasant, are strongly damped. Moreover, the fact that there is no longer any excitation of the structure means that the noise is much more localized, which is a more natural situation and therefore adds to the comfort felt.

With operation of one motor alone, governing three blinds, standardized pressure level changed from 49·9 to 39·9 dB(A).

For an overall control on the structure (eleven blinds, five motors) these values rise by only 2·5 and 1·8 dB(A).

Installation of window-shutter units

The tests conducted in the CSTB reverberation room have given the opportunity to deal with window-unit installation. Fig. 11.32 shows a 3·4 dB improvement following the insertion of an elastic mastic seal between the frame and the partitions which support them.

The final improvement on installation in real conditions is usually greater, because the power radiated is practically proportional to the surface of the vibrating panel, in this case

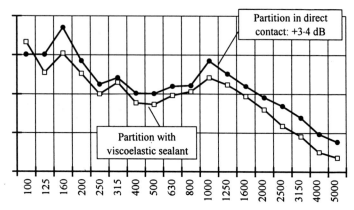

Fig. 11.32 *Effect of attaching axial suspension*

the plaster partition, which is only 5·3 m² in area. This area takes account only of 2·2 m of partition. If the width is doubled—and therefore the surface with it—an improvement of over 6 dB(A) will result when a viscoelastic mastic is used.

Part three   Recommendations

12

Product design

Incorporation of noise control parameters

Let us take an example from the motor vehicle industry. A report published by Renault[19] shows that on average 20 kg of sound insulation material must be added to the vehicle's mass for each reduction of 3 dB(A) in interior sound level (Fig. 12.1). Manufacturers estimate that comfort and safety features account for 10–15% of the mass of a vehicle. In this field it is difficult to separate with certainty the safety and sound insulation roles of some materials.

For a light class I2 car such as a Renault Clio, damping of vibrations in the dashboard metal, the front and rear floor and rear wheel arches required 10 kg of insulation on petrol models, 14 kg on diesel versions. To this quantity must be added the

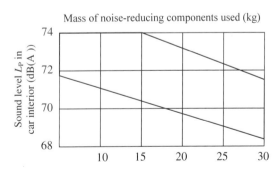

Fig. 12.1   Mass of noise-reduction components used in a car and resulting gains

large mass of the engine suspension mountings and that of the lagging under the bonnet.

Without pushing this analogy too far, it is logical for the designer/manufacturer of building services products to incorporate noise reduction principles made essential by their motorization. This is even more important in building construction, since buildings are utilized for much longer periods than a car interior.

For all the reasons cited in this work, regulations cannot impose a particular sound power level for motorized building services products, as they can for household appliances like vacuum cleaners and washing machines. The structure and fixing method are fundamental in determining the resultant sound level for the user.

However, in the same way that manufacturers of motors endeavour to reduce their sound level and vibrations, a product manufacturer will seek to reduce or eliminate effects of resonance induced or sound radiated by it and to facilitate installation in optimum conditions.

To repeat all the observations and remarks resulting from the studies described would undoubtedly be too much for the reader. Nevertheless, it is useful to gather them in the form of recommendations of the main principles for the design of such products

- avoid direct sound transmission
- prevent resonance developing in structures and sound radiation from them
- avoid vibration transmission towards support structures.

General rules

The choice of a suitable material and geometry for a product results from technical, economic, aesthetic and even historical considerations. All are perfectly legitimate and it is better not to get too involved here, except from a sound control viewpoint, by focusing on the motor tube's immediate environment.

Insulation for airborne transmission: mass of the material
We have already noted that the surface mass of the enclosing walls is an efficient damper of airborne transmission. For a closed perimeter wall, doubling the thickness improves performance by 6 dB for this kind of transmission (outside critical frequencies). Both the roller tube and the casing of the product are potentially confining walls, which we should fully exploit.

The nature of the material, for a given mass, has no bearing on this damping. The thickness required to obtain an even effect is inversely proportional to the density of the different materials, which can be a criterion for particular choices. Table 12.1 classes materials by order of decreasing density.

Table 12.1   Density of various materials

	Density: kg/m^3	Equivalent thickness for 10 kg/m^2: mm
Steel	7800	1·3
Aluminium	2700	3·7
Plywood	600	16·6
Chipboard	650	15·3
PVC	1200	8·3

Insulation for airborne transmission: composite structure
It would seem to be straightforward to provide a convenient mass in one step by the choice of the right material for the casing. However, it is also possible to take a structure of originally insufficient mass, but which gives mechanical stiffness and aesthetics to the product, and combine it with another material applied uniformly to the inside surface. The second material will therefore be one with intrinsic absorptive properties, to combine the effects of mass with those of the absorption. This leads to preference for

- rock wool (density = 30–330 kg/m³)
- open-cell polyurethane foam (density = 30 kg/m³)
- acoustic bitumen (density = 1000–2000 kg/m³)
- mixed products, such as the one shown in Fig. 12.2, especially designed for roller shutter casings.

In no case should standard polystyrene be used for sound insulation.

Open-cell foam polyurethane

Heavy viscoelastic material

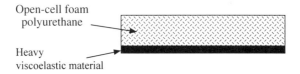

Fig. 12.2   Thick lining of sound insulation

Insulation against airborne transmission: openings
The section on Non-uniform walls in Chapter 4 has shown how openings are enemy number one of sound insulation. Ducts for passing cranking mechanisms and ventilation holes should be forbidden. However, if an opening is functionally indispensable, it should be kept as small as possible and insulated if possible. Manufacturers of ventilation intakes and hatches market products specially adapted for this.

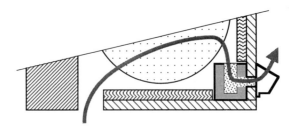

Fig. 12.3   Acoustically treated ventilation outlet

In the case of equipment that rolls and unrolls (such as screens or blinds) two blades or brushes held in light contact with the fabric can be effective insulators (Fig. 12.4).

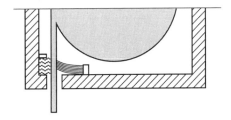

Fig. 12.4 Arrangement when a gap or slot is unavoidable

Reduction of vibrations

The choice of materials has a direct influence on the vibratory energy developed by a structure in response to a given excitation and consequently on both the sound level emitted by the structure and the strength of vibration transmitted to the supporting structures.

Intuition (and Appendix 4) indicate that there is every need for the structure to have high mechanical impedance (see the appropriate section in Chapter 1) against a build-up of excitations, which for a wall of given thickness, requires at the same time a high density and a large modulus of elasticity. If a choice of materials is available, how can they be classified? Table 12.2 indicates the mistakes to avoid. For example, if one thickness, of 10 mm, is taken as reference, steel is by far the best for fabricating a casing: three times as good as aluminium, nine times as good as concrete. Beware, however: the casing masses will be in a ratio of more than three.

What can be obtained for walls of the same mass per unit area must therefore be investigated. The value 10 kg/m^2 has been taken for the example. This corresponds to a thickness of 1·3 mm of steel. Of the three materials, steel is in that case the least

Table 12.2   *Comparison of impedances and damping*

	Density ρ: kg/m^3	Modulus of elasticity E $\times 10^6$: N/m^2	Impedance thickness 10 mm Z: Ns/m	Impedance for M/S = 10 kg/ m^2 Z: Ns/m	Loss factor (flexural excitation) η
Steel	7800	220 000	9600	160	0·0020
Aluminium	2700	72 000	3200	440	0·0001
Lead	10 600	71 000	6300	1170	0·1500
Rubber	1100	5	17	14	0·10 to 0·80
Cork	250	30	20	320	0·2500
Plywood	600	5500	420	1170	0·0120
Chipboard	650	4600	400	950	0·0130
Massive fir	600	300	100	270	0·0250
PVC	1400	3450	500	260	0·0400
Glass	2500	62 500	2900	460	0·0050
Concrete	2300	23 000	1700	310	0·0200

suitable, after concrete, which is twice as good, and way behind aluminium whose impedance is three times that of steel.

The best material is one that combines low density and high elasticity, when compared for equal mass per unit area. The higher the impedance, the lower will be the vibration velocity at the point of application of the excitation that induces a bending wave. This wave, however, propagates in the sheet of material and dissipates to it energy, expressed by the internal loss factor. The dissipation results in damping, at varying rates, of the bending wave along the sheet. It is easy to understand that strong damping greatly compensates a higher local reactivity of the sheet to excitations (Fig. 12.5).

Unfortunately for aluminium, the last column of Table 12.2 indicates that it is a poor absorber of vibrations: 20 times as poor as steel! This property, which is remarkably good for some

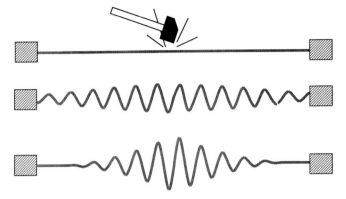

Fig. 12.5   Strong damping compensates for high reactivity

applications, is catastrophic when it is of paramount importance to avoid vibration radiation of large-size sheets subject to local excitation.

Steel, however, does not have the monopoly on virtue. Wood, concrete or even PVC, which has excellent damping properties, are preferable.

Anti-vibration treatment
Without changing the casing material, it is possible to reduce considerably its vibration level by adding viscoelastic absorbent materials. For equal efficiency, in the order of decreasing mass, these materials are

- the acoustic tars
- flexible-sheet insulators
- sandwich sheet.

Before considering these materials and applications in detail, the effectiveness of such a treatment can be judged by ear. A percussion test (Fig. 12.6) can evaluate the sound-radiation of a structure, without recourse to a vibrating pot or any other source of excitation.

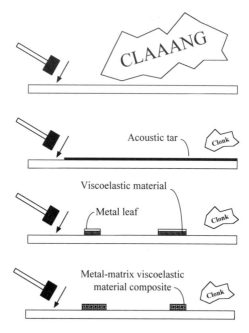

Fig. 12.6   Basic but sound test of effectiveness of materials

Acoustic tars

How do these materials act? If any viscoelastic material is set in vibration, energy is dissipated (vibratory energy is converted into thermal energy by internal friction within the material). This is the basic effect, used in acoustic bitumens. As this effect is weak, the material must be laid thickly on the vibrating sheet to obtain effective results.

The latter drawback can prove advantageous: a thicker reinforcement on the wall also produces a better insulation from airborne transmission. Moreover, this treatment is not expensive.

Flexible sheet insulators (FSI)

It is possible to increase considerably the absorption effect of the viscoelastic layer by compelling it to undergo greater deformations. Flexible sheet insulators (FSI) are therefore used, which consist of a metal matrix or, more simply, one or several superimposed metal sheets embedded in viscoelastic material.

Figure 12.7 shows how a bending vibration of the support sheet also causes flexion of the metal sheets it carries, which produces considerable shearing of the viscoelastic layer. Owing to their good performance these insulators need only partially cover the surface to be treated for vibrations (Fig. 12.6).

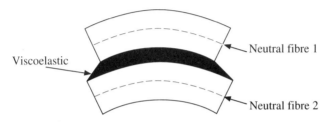

Fig. 12.7   *Increased efficiency of viscoelastic material brought by shearing*

Sandwich sheets (VDSS)
Also known as composite sheets (or vibration damping steel sheet—VDSS), the sandwich sheets carry the concept of viscoelastic damping by a shearing constraint to completion. The sheet consists of an extremely thin coat of viscoelastic polymer (45 μm) between two steel sheets 0·35–1 mm thick, giving a total thickness of 0·75–2·05 mm. The idea is an old one, but it is only in the last decade that Nippon Steel, in Japan, and Sollac, in Europe, have really resolved all the technological problems of producing such sheets on an industrial scale (Fig. 12.9).

Fig. 12.8   *Sandwich sheet*

The sheets can be pre-coated, are pliable and can be point-soldered electrically. This type of sheet arrangement can reasonably be expected to be utilized frequently for the applications considered in this book, being even more suitable for those than for the car industry targeted by the manufacturers.

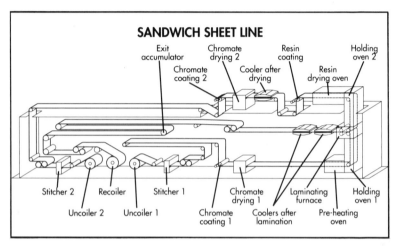

SANDWICH SHEET LINE

Fig. 12.9   *Production line of Solconfort^{TM} sandwich sheets (from Sollac^{TM} document)*

Viscoelastic coupling
It has been seen that a viscoelastic transmission effectively minimizes, as close as possible to the source, the propagation of vibrations towards the roller and towards the fixing points on to the structure. This kind of transmission is easier to make if the torque to be transmitted is weak, which is an advantage because the interior products, acoustically more sensitive, are also those with the lowest power.

It is evident that a viscoelastic coupling between the output shaft and the drive wheel works well only when used

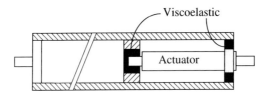

Fig. 12.10   Viscoelastic transmission

simultaneously with a viscoelastic annulus, linked to the revolution-counter bearing.

The transmission is effective only if designed in the right dimensions, according to the rules mentioned in Chapter 7. In particular, the inertia of the driven element must be high enough to minimize coupling phenomena which take away the transmission's filtering efficiency.

Viscoelastic suspension

The arrangement of the product can make a viscoelastic suspension of the motor tube preferable to a viscoelastic transmission between the motor and the tube. (One might also wish to combine the two!)

The suspension is only effective if produced in the right size, according to the rules indicated in Chapter 7. In particular, the mass of the supporting structure (or its rigidity) must be high enough to minimize coupling phenomena which remove the suspension's filtering efficiency.

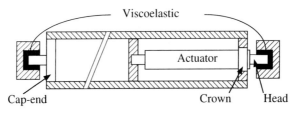

Fig. 12.11   Viscoelastic suspension

Geometry of the roller or of the casing

Concerning vibrations, a circular section is always preferable to a rectangular or polygonal section. The circular shape avoids the numerous flexural modes otherwise possible when plates are assembled together (Fig. 12.12).

These concepts are widely used in ventilation ducts. When a rectangular section is required stiffening hoops are used. It is useful to aim to reproduce this type of arrangement for rollers and casings of products considered here.

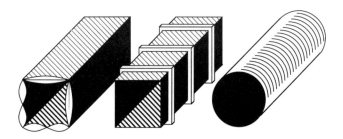

Fig. 12.12   Different geometries of permitted flexure[2]

Specific products

Combination window-shutter

Prefabricated window units are highly integrated modular products. For their manufacturers this gives an advantage in the independence of their acoustic properties from installation conditions, so that their characteristics can be easily determined.

The PVC window-unit does not invite any particular comment, except that the example given in Chapter 10 shows clearly that it is possible to obtain excellent results when the product is well designed and that the strong impedance and high damping coefficient of this material are exploited. This allows a large reduction of solid-borne sound transmission. Only techniques for airborne-transmission insulation would be necessary to obtain even more satisfactory results in particularly severe conditions.

The aluminium window-unit studied and described in chapter 10 shows that excellent performances can be obtained with this material, which would not at first be thought suitable, on condition that the casing is not in contact with the rest of the framework and its internal faces are lined by a thin layer of FSI insulator.

In all cases the ventilation aperture, if there is one, will be inserted in the window framework and not in the framework of the casing. The shutter unrolling slot will be reduced to a strict minimum and possibly fitted with two rubber blades.

Traditional roller shutter in internal casing
The casing will be constructed using the maximum thickness compatible with the conditions and cost. A close fit of the front face against the side panels is essential and possible sound leaks will be prevented by a sealing mastic. All these recommendations go along with good thermal insulation. The latter is sometimes neglected when the casing serves as a ventilation passage, a situation to be prevented for acoustic reasons, unless suitably lined air vents are used on the internal face.

The thermal insulation lining the internal faces of the casing will preferably be in rock wool, or any thermal insulator with known acoustic properties, and never in expanded polystyrene.

Roller shutter in renovated modular casing
Roller shutters in a renovated casing do not cause any great noise problems, because they are attached to the outside of the building. However, it is still advantageous to arrange for sound damping when windows are open, in the summer for instance, using FSI or by making the casing in sandwich sheets to limit its vibrations.

Using a low-stiffness fixture of the monobloc shutter on the runners will make any elastic suspension on the motor tube ineffective.

Roller shutters in lintel casing
A lintel casing gives optimum acoustic efficiency if a cladding in fibralite and not in polystyrene is used. The casing flanges will be fixtures in rigid or heavy materials such as concrete. Because the whole of the structure is joined to the masonry, flanges which are too flexible will not prevent the solid transmission of vibrations to the concrete and they will impair the efficiency of any viscoelastic suspension of the motor tube

Venetian blinds
Venetian blind casings are usually made in thin, flexible steel, placed on three sides only. This increases vibration problems. For noise control, a closed structure with four stiffened faces (and two end caps) greatly improves defences against airborne transmission. The casing sound radiation will be markedly reduced by using FSI, or by manufacture in sandwich sheeting. Because the casing lacks stiffness, suspension of the motor tube inside the casing to prevent vibrations is not a realistic option, unless the suspension point can be made to coincide with the attachment point with the wall, which in turn must be heavy or rigid.

This succession of 'unless-and-on-condition-that' factors indicates how difficult it is to design an acoustically correct product. Logically, the casing should be kept completely out of contact with the roller, which should be fixed to a solid structure, as Fig. 12.13 suggests.

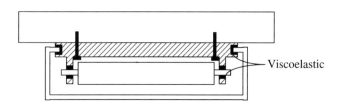

Fig. 12.13   Venetian blind arrangement designed to minimize noise

Screens

Most of the statements made concerning venetian blinds can be applied to film projection screens, with even more relevance since the high sensitivity of an audience to the sound level of this type of product has to be considered, as mentioned in the introduction to Chapter 8.

Screens are most often arranged in an extruded-aluminium casing much stiffer than that for venetian blinds, but which nevertheless necessitates a partial covering of the internal faces with an FSI material which will constitute the basic treatment.

If it is desirable to really keep the decibels at bay

- the fixing braces should have sufficient mass and stiffness for the assembly to benefit from the addition of a viscoelastic device
- the roller should be made perfectly silent by arranging an elastic coupling on the drive mechanism and a flexible wheel at the revolution-counter bearing
- viscoelastic studs should be used to fix the rods for hanging the product to the ceiling slab; these are placed between the upper end of the rods and the slab.

13

Installation of products

Influence of installation conditions

The results reported in Chapter 11 show the large improvements that can be achieved by taking noise problems into account in the installation of products in buildings. The designer of such products will strive for an arrangement that avoids such problems and will issue to installers recommendations enabling them to combat effectively sound leakage (by airborne transmission), vibration transmission on heavy structures (solid-borne transmission) and solid excitation of lightweight walls and partitions. This chapter briefly covers these recommendations.

Sound leaks

The question of sound leaks was mentioned in Chapter 12 (under the section on General rules) in relation to the general design of casings. Installation proper concerns mainly roller shutters placed in an internally-mounted box. Fig. 13.1 shows how leaks occur.

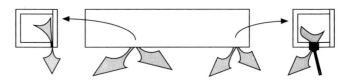

Fig. 13.1   Leakage: all it needs is a small gap . . .

It is the responsibility of the installer of the product to

● ensure that woodwork and framework are airtight
● ensure that any remaining space is plugged by a sound-proofing sealant, or at least by a standard heat-insulation mastic.

If the roller shutter is equipped with a handle for stand-by manual control, special attention should be paid to prevent sound leakage from gaps where parts of the mechanism pass through to connect with the roller. As manual control would seldom be used, the unit could even be sealed off completely, if the sealant used (silicone) allows the shaft of the mechanism to be pivoted. The reduction ratio of the winching system is enough for the extra stress caused by this friction to be negligible.

In the case of venetian blinds, or some screens, a casing is often partially masked by a woodwork panel to conceal it when completely raised. Such a panel will help in sound insulation only if it is 'float' mounted on the ceiling, suspended or fixed with a flexible joint, and covered by an absorbent on the interior face. All contact with the product casing must be avoided (Fig. 13.2).

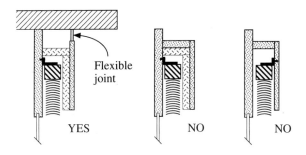

Fig. 13.2 Rational use of a concealment panel

Fixing to a heavy structure

As a matter of principle, a product should always be fixed on to a solid wall (in poured concrete, breeze-blocks, brick and plaster). Vibrations transmitted to the heavy wall do not generate any significant sound emission directly from it.

However, any light structure joined to this heavy wall will in its turn be excited by vibrations propagated in the wall. Thus the unexpected problem can arise of a high sound level inside the room or space where the device has been installed (source room or space) or in a neighbouring room or space (receiving room or space), even though the equipment has been attached to a solid structure. This situation is encountered notably when internal plaster and polystyrene facing panels are used, or, for example, with walls clad with wooden panelling.

One extremely effective answer to this consists of using a viscoelastic fixture to mount the product on the heavy structure (Fig. 13.3). It is the job of the manufacturers of the products and of the motors used with them to make such fittings available to the installers, possibly along with charts which allow a choice depending on the mass of the product.

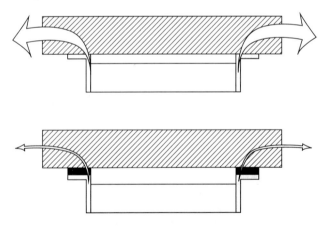

Fig. 13.3   Effective weapon against solid-borne transmission

Use of a viscoelastic suspension for a product on a heavy wall ensures a considerable reduction of solid-borne transmission towards adjoining rooms.

Beware of direct contact
Like an electrical short-circuit, any direct contact, even far from the suspension point, spoils the suspension's effect, by diverting the greater part of the solid-borne transmission: insulation is either total or completely ineffective (Fig. 13.4).

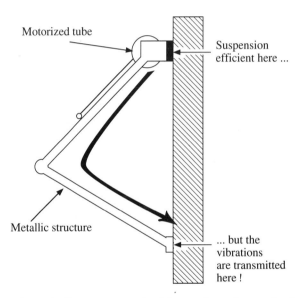

Fig. 13.4 *Wasted effort: suspension fitted for one fixture but not for the other*

Beware of abutting lightweight structures
In the case where the product is installed on a heavy wall, the fitter should take care that lightweight partitions or panels do not abut directly on any part of the product. This is a very common mistake.

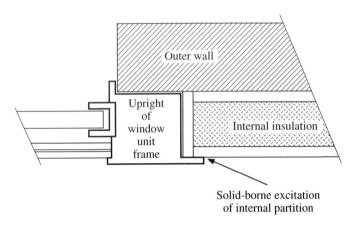

Fig. 13.5 Precautions necessary for window-unit installation

The case of side panels which conceal a venetian blind or a cinema screen has already been mentioned. It has also been known in modular combinations for a window-shutter, in contact with the plaster-composite panel used to clad the inside of the façades (Fig. 13.5). A sound-proofing sealant will be used in this case, as generally recommended, as an intermediate layer between the window-unit and the interior wall skin. This recommendation is particularly relevant for aluminium window-blocks, which permit more solid transmission than other types.

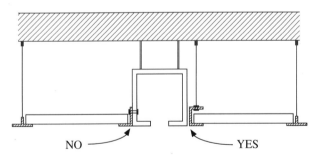

Fig. 13.6 Direct abutment of false ceiling to be avoided

The same recommendation applies to cinema screens for conference rooms and lecture theatres. They are usually flush-fitted in the false ceilings (Fig. 13.6).

Fixing to a lightweight wall or partition

Attachment of a product to a lightweight wall or partition (has to withstand the weight of the product) is usually easy for the fitter, it being easier to drill wood than solid concrete, but catastrophic for noise control. It is therefore vital to recommend that, whenever possible, products are always fixed on a heavy structure (Fig. 13.7).

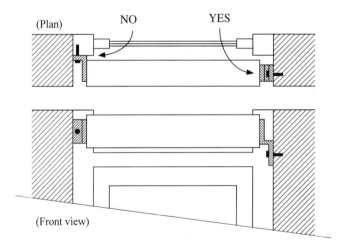

Fig. 13.7 Attachment must be on solid structure, not on lightweight framework

However, lightweight partitions or panelling are sometimes unavoidable. If equipment of given characteristics, has to be mounted on a lightweight structure, the fitter should be reminded that a viscoelastic device will have no effect, or could

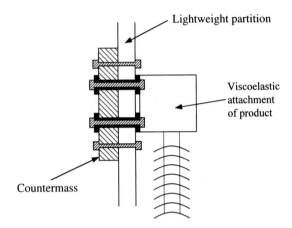

Fig. 13.8   Countermass used to make viscoelastic device more effective

even worsen vibrations set up in the structure. Nevertheless, if it is possible to place a countermass at the same level as the fixing point the virtues of viscoelastic suspension can be rediscovered.

14

Consequences for architectural design

Architecture and the active façade

The use of variable shading systems gives the architect an extra degree of freedom in the design of building façades which, like the biological envelope of a living organism, can adapt naturally to the circadian and seasonal rhythms. The combination of criteria concerned purely with energy with those for heating and lighting comfort gives rise to buildings in which aesthetic feats vie with architectural challenge (Figs 14.1 and 14.3).

Although it is not the central topic of this work, we highlight here the important factors which will make the active façade one of the great architectural themes of the twenty-first century. Such a feature is not just a fashion: it follows on logically from extensive thought on comfort and the overall economic aspects of building projects.

Figure 14.2 shows how temperature changes in a room of 35 m^3 volume, ventilated normally, with a 2 m^2 window in the roof. The location is at Trappes, near Paris, and the time is a day in July. The upper curve describes what happens when the shading blind is not deployed, the lower one is for when the shading is kept unfurled. The middle curve shows how an automatic mechanism controlling the degree of opening of the shading gives a good amount of light in the room (600 lux at the measuring point) and considerably reduces summer overheating.

It is this kind of consideration, coupled with a now common realization of the vagaries of glass architecture, that explains the

Fig. 14.1   BPO building (courtesy of SOMFY, Architects: Odile Decq and Benoît Cornette)

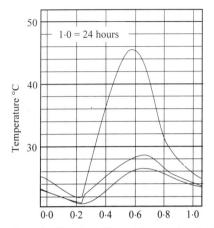

Fig. 14.2   Control of heating effect with an active façade element

Fig. 14.3   Elements for building environment control (BPO building) (courtesy of SOMFY)

development of automatic equipment for the mobile envelope on buildings.[20] This development owes much to the reduction in maintenance costs brought by motorization of equipment.

Whether as equipment separate from or incorporated in a factory-assembled façade element, automated products for closing up, for solar protection or for darkening, will eventually become commonplace. It is therefore highly advantageous for an architect, now well versed in the related but sometimes contradictory technologies of thermal insulation and traditional sound insulation (road noise, insulation between units in a building, noise from collective building services plant) to be able to choose the best solutions to combat noise in terms of products and installation conditions.

The best choices

An upstream element of the project
Although light building services equipment appears chronologically in the second stage of building works, we reiterate how much effect choices in this domain have on the energy budget of the building and on the control of heating and lighting conditions, factors which should truly be considered upstream if there are any.

Incorporation of these elements into the façade in the early design stages will contribute to the aesthetics and original appearance of the building. Similarly, the choice of supporting structures and volumes will influence the chances of obtaining a near-faultless acoustic performance of mobile-envelope equipment.

Internal or external equipment?
When the overall design of the façade allows, it is of course preferable to use products fitted externally or enclosed in a double skin. This goes for both acoustic and thermal benefits. This does not mean that the numerous interior products available should be avoided, as they have the advantage of

great flexibility and generally lower costs, but rather that they need special care for sound control (aided, it is true, by lower power levels at work).

As for airborne transmission, benefit is then gained from the insulation afforded by the façade (D_n greater than 30 dB(A)), which is ample in all situations.

The advantage brought by installing equipment outside should not be lost by allowing a direct solid-borne transmission to the framework or glazing.

Anchorage on heavy walls

Independently of the ability of the structure to support the weight of the enclosing or solar-protection equipment, a solid wall or surface as an anchoring point for motorized elements ensures that there will be no direct emission by the wall and that a viscoelastic device fixed at the attachment point will be effective (Fig. 14.4). Recourse to an indirect attachment by this kind of fixture will be necessary if the heavy wall also supports lightweight elements that could take on a high vibration velocity when the heavy wall itself vibrates.

Fig. 14.4   Direct anchorage on heavy wall (field test 6)

Anchorage on rigid structures

It is often necessary to make the attachment on to a metal support structure, which is not favourable acoustically. A tubular structure, which is more common, is the type that gives the best performance.

It is essential for the structure to be rigid at the anchorage point for the motorized product. Once again it is a condition if any viscoelastic device is to work properly, to avoid excitation of the structure by the equipment. In the example shown in Fig. 14.5 fixing on the outside has made superfluous any device to

Fig. 14.5   BPO building: fixing detail (courtesy of SOMFY)

avoid direct contact. However, the structure used, whose main job is to hold up the curtain of glass, would be stiff enough for such suspensions to be effective.

In this set-up, the glass sheets are not set in vibration by the external structure, owing probably to a viscoelastic device used to anchor them in place (Fig. 14.6).

Light walls and low-stiffness structures

It is from the design stage that steps must be taken to avoid all direct contact between a motorized element and a structure of low stiffness or a lightweight wall or partition (glazing, metal or

Fig. 14.6   BPO building: attachment to glass curtain (courtesy of SOMFY)

timber framework, lightweight veneers, facings, false ceilings and so on).

Group control
Even stricter precautions should be taken if simultaneous activation and control is envisaged for a large number of elements of equipment in a given building volume (foyers, concert halls, museums, etc).

Regulations

Noise regulations have been covered in Chapter 5, where the examples of Switzerland (the standard SIA 181) and France (New Sound Regulations—Nouvelle Réglementation Acoustique (NRA)) were mentioned. As far as the equipment in question is concerned the latter rules only confirm older texts. It is more the general climate and the attention given by public authorities that give these documents their value. We have therefore entered an era where acoustic considerations of the end user of the building are widely, and justly, taken on board.

It was noted in Chapter 5 that, although the French regulations appeared more strict than their British or Swiss counterparts for this type of product (with a limit set at L_n of 30 dB(A)), the corrective figure of 9 dB introduced in the code of specific tests makes the effective level of 39 dB(A) perfectly accessible, even in the case of group control of enclosing or screening products in one flat or unit. Example 5.4 has shown besides that, to the nearest decibel, we arrive at the same required limit of sound power on both sides of the border. All the examples and descriptions of field tests given show that the strictest limits are met, provided that products and their installation conditions have been well chosen for a building which itself incorporates noise-control considerations.

It would indeed have been surprising to find the opposite. Standards are set to incite a general improvement, by imposing limits that are strict but accessible.

Shared tasks and interacting roles

What the architect expects, in the same way as his client or the various end-users involved, is to be able to guarantee good acoustic performance of the final result and working tools in order to make the best choice of products and their application.

In a short but invaluable booklet entitled *NRA—Exemple de Solutions Acoustiques/NRA—Example of Acoustic Solutions*, the CSTB sets out the framework of measures associating the components with the solutions. The components are classified by type (AC0, AC1, AC2 . . .) in order of increasing sound and vibratory performance. Classification of a component in a given category results either from certification, or from a standard test done less than five years beforehand, or in some cases even from a straightforward physical description of the component.

Depending on the architecture, good acoustic design can use components with different properties, taking account of the end use of the spaces concerned. Two examples are

- an individual heater must be classified AC2 if placed in a main room or in a kitchen that opens out to a living room, but as AC1 if it is in a closed kitchen
- lift machinery must be separated from adjacent flats by a BA22 wall covered with a type AC2 lining if the next room is a main room, or AC1 if it is a utility room.

There we have well-illustrated measures which will become more comprehensive as successive improvements are made. Our common studies will combine to establish them for motorized lightweight equipment products for buildings. Soon, in this same area, architects will therefore be guided towards a choice of AC2 or AC1 products depending on the architectural solution they are preparing to put into practice.

Soon, because in spite of all the data already available—and this book is a reflection of that—the different products and varied installation conditions possible, and the novelty of the subject will make things more complicated than is the case for components currently presented as an aid to design according to the NRA regulations.

But a manufacturer of these motorized products for building services, who incorporates all these factors, will not be indifferent to such measures. In defining the test code, the assessment criteria, solutions to sound problems and so on, a whole profession is mobilized to make available not only good products, but also suitable tools to enable choices to be made by the architects who combine them in their designs. Correct information given on product characteristics and performance is always favourable to those who make the effort to improve them.

Appendix 1

Relations between sound pressure, intensity and power

Propagation of plane waves

Equations relating to wave propagation in a gas, and therefore in air, are established[1,21] from the Euler equation (the equivalent of Newton's law $F = m\gamma$), a continuity equation which expresses the conservation of mass, and a hypothesis that the changes dP of pressure P and dV of volume V occur without heat exchange with the exterior (an adiabatic situation), which is expressed by opposite changes

$$\frac{dP}{P} = -\gamma \frac{dV}{V} \tag{A1.1}$$

The coefficient $\gamma (\gamma = C_p/C_v)$ for air is 1·4.

When one-directional plane waves are propagated, it is shown the following.

- These waves propagate with a wave speed c which depends only on absolute temperature T (in Kelvins) and the physical parameters of the gas: the molar mass M and the constant R for perfect gases

$$c = \left(\frac{\gamma RT}{M}\right)^{1/2} \tag{A1.2}$$

The ratio R/M is 287 J/(kgK) for air, or approximately

$$c = 20\sqrt{T} \tag{A1.3}$$

which gives 330 m/s at 0°C and 342 m/s at 20°C.

- The air particles move from one side of their equilibrium position to the other with an oscillatory displacement s and the alternating particle velocity v is $90°$ shifted in phase with s (one is zero when the other is maximum).
- The instantaneous changes in pressure, denoted p, are proportional to the local variations of density ρ

$$p = c^2 \rho \qquad (A1.4)$$

These variations are in phase with those of the particle velocity. The ratio between the pressure variations and the velocity, which is constant with time, is denoted by Z, the characteristic impedance of air

$$Z = \frac{p}{v} = \rho_0 c \quad \text{or} \quad p = \rho_0 c v \qquad (A1.5)$$

where ρ_0 is the density of air. Z is about 400 Nsm^{-3} at 0°C.

Sound pressure and intensity for a plane wave
In acoustics the instantaneous power is denoted by $w(t)$. It corresponds to particle motion. This power is equal to the product of the force exerted on the particles (here resulting from the pressure) by their displacement velocity

$$w(t) = f(t)v(t) = p(t)Sv(t) \qquad (A1.6)$$

where S is the surface area of the plane wave considered. The instantaneous sound intensity $i(t)$ is equal to the power propagated per unit area

$$i(t) = \frac{w(t)}{S} = p(t)v(t) = [(v(t))^2(\rho_0 c)] = \left[\frac{(p(t))^2}{(\rho_0 c)} \right] \qquad (A1.7)$$

with relation (A1.5) taken into account. The average value of intensity in time $i(t)$ is I and that of $(p(t))^2$ is P^2. P is the effective value of the pressure (the square of the effective value of a quantity is the time mean of the square of this quantity). One obtains therefore

$$I = \frac{P^2}{(\rho_0 c)} = \frac{P^2}{400} \qquad (A1.8)$$

If reference values I_{ref} and P_{ref} are taken such that

$$I_{ref} = \frac{P_{ref}}{400} \qquad (A1.9)$$

one obtains

$$\frac{I}{I_{ref}} = \left(\frac{P}{P_{ref}}\right)^2 \qquad (A.10)$$

or, by taking 10 times the logarithm of this expression, to obtain the levels (dB)

$$L_I = L_P \qquad (A1.11)$$

Propagation of spherical wave
In the case of a spherical wave, propagating from a point source, it can be shown that the speed of the waves does not change in comparison with the preceding case and that the same proportionality exists between changes in pressure and in density. However, relation (A1.5) holds only for a distance from the source which is much larger than the wavelength. It is shown that p and v are 90° phase-shifted with the immediate vicinity of the source. At a long enough distance from the source, the behaviour of a spherical wave becomes analogous with that of a plane wave.

Sound pressure and intensity for a spherical wave
At a sufficiently large distance r from the source, expression (A1.8), which gives the intensity I, can be used. Multiplication of I by the surface area S of the sphere of radius r, gives the total power carried by the wave. If the propagation occurs without any loss, this power is equal to the average power W supplied by the source to create the initial wave

$$W = IS = I4\pi r^2 \tag{A1.12}$$

$$P^2 = \frac{W\rho_0 c}{(4\pi r^2)} \tag{A1.13}$$

If one or more reflectors are present the apparent power of the source can change in the portion of space where propagation occurs. This is expressed by a multiplication factor of directivity Q.

In free-field conditions, i.e. with no obstacle to propagation of waves from the source

$$P^2 = \frac{W\rho_0 cQ}{(4\pi r^2)} \tag{A1.14}$$

Diffuse (reverberated) field
The situation is a large reverberation room containing a source of power W. After a time, wherever the observation point is, an observer will find a multitude of plane waves which correspond to the reflections, from all possible angles of incidence, of the waves on the walls. Considering the large dimensions of the room, these can be taken to be plane waves.

At any point, therefore, there is an equal probability of finding a plane wave propagating in every direction in the space. An intensimeter will give

$$I = 0 \qquad\qquad (A1.15)$$

In a reverberating field the sound intensity is zero at any point: as much passes in one direction as in another.

A plane sensor that only takes into account the waves which cross it in a given direction is placed at M in Fig. A1.1. If this direction is from right to left for instance, each elementary plane wave, of average intensity i, coming from a direction θ, contributes to the total intensity measured in the direction perpendicular to the plane of the sensor, by a value $i\cos\theta$. All the contributions having a given value of θ and perpendicular to the plane of the sensor add up, whereas those parallel to the plane cancel each other out.

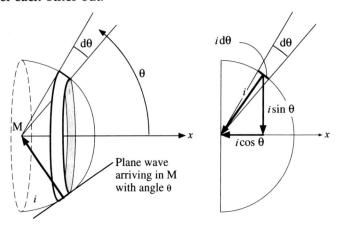

Fig. A1.1   *Integration of resultant intensity on 1/2 space*

In the neighbourhood of a direction identified by the angle θ in relation to 0_x, a number of vectors are found proportional to the portion dS of the sphere surface S (shaded in Fig. A1.1), owing to the equiprobable distribution. This proportion is

$$\frac{dS}{S} = (2\pi i \sin\theta)\left(\frac{i d\theta}{4\pi i^2}\right) = \tfrac{1}{2}\sin\theta d\theta \qquad\qquad (A1.16)$$

All these vectors have the same intensity component i_x depending on direction 0_x

$$i_x = i \cos \theta \tag{A1.17}$$

For a neighbourhood $d\theta$, around direction θ, the sum of the components of all these vectors is therefore

$$\tfrac{1}{2} i \cos \theta \sin \theta d\theta = \tfrac{1}{4} id(\cos^2 \theta) \tag{A1.18}$$

When all the contributions are added up, with θ varying from 0 to 90°, a total intensity I' is obtained which comes from the half-space considered, equal to

$$I' = \frac{i}{4} = \frac{P^2}{(4\rho_0 c)} \tag{A1.19}$$

The fact that in a diffuse field a value 4 times weaker is found than for a field of plane waves in the same direction is expressed by a loss of 6 dB from the intensity level

$$L_I = L_{P'} - 6 \tag{A1.20}$$

Power losses by absorption on the walls are proportional to the incident intensity I' and to the walls' absorption coefficient α. If the total surface area of the walls is now denoted S, the average power W_a absorbed on these is

$W_a = I'S\alpha = I'A$

$A = \alpha S$ = equivalent absorption area or Sabine absorption

$$\tag{A1.21}$$

The sound level in the room ceases to grow when this absorbed power W_a compensates the power W supplied by the source. In diffuse-field conditions, the relation linking the average pressure P to the average power of the source is written

$$P^2 = \frac{4W\rho_0 c}{A} \qquad \text{(A1.22)}$$

Resultant field
When a direct field and a reverberated field occur simultaneously, the resultant pressure at an instant is the sum of the contributions of pressure from each, p_d and p_r

$$p(t) = p_d(t) + p_r(t) \qquad \text{(A1.23)}$$

$$(p(t))^2 = (p_d(t))^2 + (p_r(t))^2 + 2(p_d(t))(p_r(t)) \qquad \text{(A1.24)}$$

The average over time of the doubled product will give zero because the two terms do not show any phase coherence. The following is obtained

$$P^2 = P_d{}^2 + P_r{}^2 \qquad \text{(A1.25)}$$

or

$$P^2 = W\rho_0 c \left(\frac{Q}{(4\pi r^2)} + \frac{4}{A} \right) \qquad \text{(A1.26)}$$

Appendix 2

The Sabine formula (1900)

Energy of plane waves propagating in a volume V
We take a field of plane waves moving in the same direction with speed c. These waves cross a section S perpendicular to the direction of propagation. The sound energy E contained in a parallelepiped volume V, delimited by S and of length L, crosses S after a time $t = L/c$. This gives

$$E = ISt = \frac{IV}{c} \tag{A2.1}$$

This same relation is obtained by observing that the total energy is the sum of the kinetic and potential energies of the air particles, quantities which are equal in a sinusoidal oscillatory motion

$$E = 2(\tfrac{1}{2}mv^2)_{av} = (mv^2)_{av} = \rho_0 V(v^2)_{av} \tag{A2.2}$$

where $_{av}$ means average value, and by applying (A1.5) also to express v as a function of p

$$E = \frac{V(p^2)_{av}}{(\rho_0 c^2)} \tag{A2.3}$$

$$E = \frac{IV}{c} \tag{A2.4}$$

Energy of reverberated plane waves
In the diffuse field, made up of waves that are reflected in all directions, relation A2.2 still allows the stationary energy contained in the volume V to be calculated: it gives the result in A2.3.

We have seen in Appendix A that intensity I is zero, because at all points in the volume will be found as many waves circulating in opposite directions as in any one direction. However, the result A2.3 can be expressed as a function of the intensity I' of incident waves coming from a half-space

$$E = \frac{V(p^2)_{av}}{(\rho_0 c^2)} = \frac{4I'V}{c} \qquad \text{(A2.5)}$$

Energy balance in a reverberation room
The reverberation room is supposed to contain a source that supplies a constant average power W. During a time interval dt the sound energy of the room increases by Wdt. There should therefore be uniform growth in sound energy in the course of time.

However, the walls dissipate energy. If W_a is the power absorbed by the walls, the energy lost in the same time interval is $W_a dt$. The overall balance is

$$dE = Wdt - W_a dt \quad \text{or} \quad \frac{dE}{dt} = W - W_a \qquad \text{(A2.6)}$$

It is observed that if the power of a source is constant, the same does not apply to the power W_a absorbed by the wall which is greater the higher the incident intensity I' on the walls (A1.21). We obtain

$$\frac{dE}{dt} = \frac{4V}{c}\frac{dI'}{dt} = W - AI' \qquad \text{(A2.7)}$$

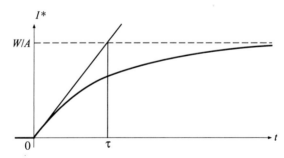

Fig. A2.1   Sound intensity (or pressure) determination

$$\frac{\mathrm{d}I'}{\mathrm{d}t} = -\frac{I'}{\tau} + \frac{W}{(A\tau)} \tag{A2.8}$$

with $\tau = \dfrac{4V}{(Ac)}$ = the room's time constant $\tag{A2.9}$

The differential equation A2.8, encountered in numerous physical equilibrium processes, shows that such equilibrium is reached when $I' = W/A$, seeing that in that case $\mathrm{d}I'/\mathrm{d}t = 0$. In physical terms, this means that the power supplied by the source is equal to that dissipated by the walls.

Figure A2.1 shows how sound intensity or pressure is established. When the source is switched on in an initially silent room, integrating the equation gives

$$I' = \frac{W}{A}(1 - e^{-t/\tau}) \tag{A2.10}$$

The same time course is found for pressure. After a time τ the value obtained is 63% of the final one. After 3τ and 5τ it is 95 and 99%. Similarly, once the source is switched off, these quantities decrease exponentially

$$I' = \frac{W}{A}e^{-t/\tau} \tag{A2.11}$$

As for these quantities expressed as levels, the decrease appears to be linear (Fig. A2.3).

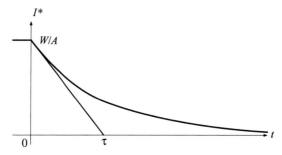

Fig. A2.2   Fall-off in sound intensity (or pressure)

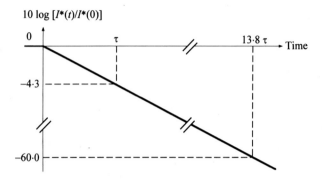

$10 \log [I^*(t)/I^*(0)]$

Fig. A2.3   Decrease in level after switching off source, in dB

The quantity T_R is defined by the following relation: if $t = T_R$, $E = E_0/10^6$. So

$$T_R = \tau ln\ 10^6 = 6\tau\ ln\ 10 = \frac{552\ V}{Ac} \qquad (A2.12)$$

$$T_R = \frac{016V}{A} \quad (\text{if } c = 340\ m/s) \qquad (A2.13)$$

Instead of using the reverberation time, a relationship can be obtained with the decay rate d which indicates (units: dB/s) the time rate at which the sound level decreases in the room

$$d = \frac{60}{T_R} \qquad (A2.14)$$

Then, from A2.12 comes

$$A = \frac{092Vd}{c} \qquad (A2.15)$$

Appendix 3

Transmission of sound power through a wall

Figure A3.1 shows a separation partition, of area S. Here are specified the conditions required to determine a sound loss index for the partition.

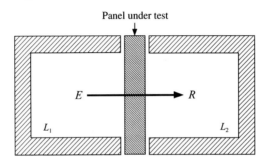

Fig. A3.1   *Transmission through a partition or wall*

It is assumed there is a diffuse field, in both the source room R1 and the receiving room R2. The incident intensity I_1' in room R1 on partition S is therefore given by relation A1.19

$$I_1' = \frac{P_1^2}{(4\rho_0 c)} \tag{A3.1}$$

The power W_t transmitted to room R2 by the partition is equal to the product of the incident power and the transmission coefficient t

$$W_t = t I_1' S \tag{A3.2}$$

For R2 this power is the source of the sound power W_2. (This reasoning is used systematically in the 'SEA' method: the energy transmitted from one side is considered as the source for the other.)

Therefore

$$W_2 = tI_1'S \tag{A3.3}$$

As R2 is considered as a reverberation room, A2.22 is applied

$$P_2{}^2 = \frac{4W_2 \rho_0 c}{A_2} \tag{A3.4}$$

This is combined with the preceding relations

$$P_2{}^2 = \frac{tP_1{}^2 S}{A_2} \tag{A3.5}$$

$$\left(\frac{P_2}{P_{\text{ref}}}\right)^2 = t\left(\frac{P_1}{P_{\text{ref}}}\right)^2 \frac{S}{A_2} \tag{A3.6}$$

$$L_{P_2} = 10 \log t + L_{P_1} + 10 \log \frac{S}{A_2} \tag{A3.7}$$

$$R = 10 \log \frac{1}{t} = -10 \log t = L_{P_1} - L_{P_2} + 10 \log \frac{S}{A_2} \tag{A3.8}$$

. . . this is why the equivalent absorption area of the receiving room is included in determinations of the loss index of a wall or partition.

Appendix 4

Vibration of and radiation from structures

To study this topic in depth, specialist literature should be referred to, especially references 21 and 22. Only certain terms and formulas used in the main body of the book are given here. Beware: except in the last section, we take up the mechanics notation again—P for power, W for energy.

Modes of some structures
Elongated tubular beam in (mutually supporting) arrangement

$$f_i = \left(\frac{i^2\pi}{8L^2}\right)\left[\frac{E(D_{ext^2} + D_{int^2})}{\rho}\right]^{1/2} \tag{A4.1}$$

where i is the order of the mode, which is a whole number; L is the length of the tube; D_{ext} and D_{int} are diameters of the tube; ρ is the density; E is the modulus of elasticity.

Ring frequency of a tube of radius r

$$f = \frac{1}{2\pi r}\sqrt{\frac{E}{\rho}} \tag{A4.2}$$

Loss factor
The loss factor η expresses the extent of losses in a structure subject to excitement of frequency f. By definition

$$\eta = \frac{\Delta W}{(2\pi W)} \tag{A4.3}$$

where ΔW is the energy dissipated per period and W is the total vibration (or other) energy of the structure. The loss factor is usually measured around the resonance of the structure (Fig. A4.1), starting from its frequency response.

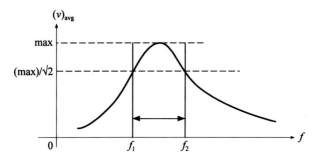

Fig. A4.1 Determination of loss factor

The loss factor η and the damping rate ε represent the same phenomenon ($\eta = 2\varepsilon$). The smaller they are, the higher the resonance for a given frequency f_n. The following is obtained

$$\eta = \frac{(f_2 - f_1)}{f_n} \qquad (A4.4)$$

Q, the inverse of the loss factor, is the quality coefficient of the structure.

In the case of a vibrating plate, losses occur inside the material, resulting from the radiation of the plate in air and from conduction of the vibration energy at the contacts between the plate and other elements

$$\eta = \eta_i + \eta_r + \eta_c \qquad (A4.5)$$

The losses by radiation are always very small.

Average vibration response of a plate excited at a point
For an extremely large plate, of thickness h, locally subjected to an alternating force (frequency f) of effective value F, the

effective vibration velocity v_0 at the point of application is shown to be F/Z. Impedance Z is

$$Z \approx \frac{4}{\sqrt{3}} h^2 \sqrt{(\rho E)} \qquad (A4.6)$$

In this case, the power P_t transmitted by the excitation source at this point has the value

$$P_t = \frac{F^2}{Z} \qquad (A4.7)$$

For a reduced motion at the application point h, ρ and E must simultaneously be as high as possible. However, the fact that a given wall mass M per unit surface area S cannot be exceeded is often a limiting factor. A formula that includes all these quantities is therefore used, as follows

$$Z \approx \left(\frac{4}{\sqrt{3}}\right) \left(\frac{M}{S}\right)^2 \sqrt{\left(\frac{E}{\rho^3}\right)} \qquad (A4.8)$$

To establish an expression for the average vibratory behaviour of the whole of the plate, it can be written that the latter's total vibration energy is

$$W = M <v^2> \qquad (A4.9)$$

where v is the effective velocity (rms) and $<\ >$ means that a spatially averaged value for the whole of the plate is taken (because of damping, the value decreases with distance from the excitation point). The problem is to minimize $<v^2>$. Let the energy supplied by the excitation source be equal to that dissipated by losses in a period T, in a permanent set-up

$$P_t T = \Delta W = 2\pi W \eta = 2\pi M <v^2> \eta \qquad (A4.10)$$

By combining expressions (A4.8 to A4.10), the following is obtained

$$<v^2> = \sqrt{3} F^2 \left[8\pi f \eta \left(\frac{M^3}{S^2}\right) \sqrt{\left(\frac{E}{\rho^3}\right)} \right] \qquad (A4.11)$$

This states that, for a given surface area, and for a required mass, the material chosen must give the highest possible value for the product $\eta\sqrt{(E/\rho^3)}$.

Radiation factor

The radiation factor σ is by definition the ratio between the sound power emitted by the structure and that of a plane wave in air having the same vibration velocity. It is 1 if the coupling between the structure and air allows complete communication of the velocity from one to the particles of the other. In acoustics notation the following is obtained

$$\sigma = \frac{W}{W_0} = \frac{W}{[< v_{rms} >^2 (\rho_0 c)]} \qquad (A4.12)$$

an expression derived from A1.7.

References

1. CSTB. 1984. *REEF-Acoustique*. R. JOSSE (ed.). This treatise contains several extracts from the reference work by JOSSE R. 1972. *Notions d'acoustique*. Paris: Eyrolles (out of print).
2. SOUND RESEARCH LABORATORIES. 1988. *Noise control in building services*. A. FRY (ed.). Pergamon Press, Oxford.
3. MINISTERE DE LA SANTE ET DE L'ACTION HUMANITAIRE (France). 1992. *Les effets du bruit sur la santé*. Paris.
4. TRAILL S. 1995. Too quiet an approach to quieter homes. *Noise & Vibrations Worldwide*, 16–17 Jan. 1995.
5. FAHY F. J. 1977. Measurement of acoustic intensity using the cross-spectral density of two microphone signals. *J. Acoust. Soc. Am.*, **62**, No. 4.
6. FAHY F. J. 1995. *Sound intensity*. E. & F. Spon, London.
7. REINICHE W. L. 1986. Intensimetrische Schalleistungsermittlung bei Dampfturbosaten. *VGB Kraftwerkstech*, **66**, No. 7.
8. WILLIAMS R. G. D. and YANG S. J. 1993. Advanced techniques for noise source identification on a large generator unit. *IEEE Trans.*, **8**, No. 1.
9. NEUMANN J. *et al.* 1992. *Lärmmesspraxis am Arbeitplatz und in der Nachtbarschaft*. Expert Verlag, 7th edn.
10. RANDALL R. B. 1973. *Cepstrum analysis and gearbox fault diagnosis*. Bruel & Kjaer AN 13–150.
11. SABOT J. and BOUCHAREB A. 1988. Mechanical sources of the noise radiated by gears. *Internoise 88—Senlis, France*.
12. VILLOT M., CHAVERIAT G. and ROLAND J. 1991. Phonoscopy: an acoustical holography technique for plane structures radiating in enclosed spaces. *J. Acoust. Soc. Am.*, **1**.

13. MORLON J. 1981. *Isolation antivibratoire et antichocs.* Paulstra™: Techniques de l'ingénieur B595.

14. GARNIER B. 1994. *Isolation antivibratoire et antichocs.* Metravib RDS™: Techniques de l'ingénieur B5140/41.

15. TIMAR P. L. 1989. *Noise and Vibrations of Electrical Machines.* Elsevier.

16. INSA LABORATOIRE VIBRATIONS ET ACOUSTIQUE. 1988. *Etude INSA—SOMFY no. 2890.* L. BOUCHARD and B. GUERIN, Internal report.

17. SOMFY GMBH. 1991. *Schallpegelmessungen an einer automatisierten Filmleinwand und Versuche zur Reduzierung der Schallemissionen,* Internal report.

18. CSTB. 1992, 1994. *Etudes CSTB—SOMFY no. 291157 292171 293162.* M. VILLOT and C. MARTIN, Internal report.

19. MATHIOLON H. 1994. Projet MOSAIC: l'utilisation des tôles sandwich dans un objectif d'allègement. *Sollac-Solconfort™ symposium, Paris 1994.*

20. GRÉHANT B., TANTOT M. and JAQUET P. 1993. *Automatic light control and energy savings using external screens.* Symposium IQ93, Singapore.

21. JOUHANEAU J. 1994. *Notions élémentaires d'acoustique—Electroacoustique.* Tec & Doc Lavoisier, CNAM series, Paris.

22. LESUEUR C. 1987. *Rayonnement acoustique des structures.* Eyrolles, EDF-DER series, Paris.

Useful addresses

Sound Research Laboratories Ltd
Holbrook House, Little Waldingfield, Sudbury, Suffolk (UK)
CO10 0TH
Fax +44 1787 248420

Institute of Noise Control Engineering
P.O. Box 3200 Arlington Branch
Poughkeepsie, NY 12603 (USA)
Fax +1 914 463 0201

Institute of Sound and Vibration Research, University of Southampton
Highfield
Southampton (UK)
SO17 1BJ
Fax +44 1703 593033

Centre Scientifique et Technique du Bâtiment (CSTB)
Division Bruit et Vibrations, Etablissement de Grenoble
24, rue Joseph Fourier
F-38400 Saint-Martin-d'Hères (France)
Fax +33 76 44 20 46

An International Directory of Manufacturers, Suppliers &
Consultancies will be found in
Noise & Vibrations Worldwide, Vol. 26, No. 3, March 1995
Published by Institute of Physics Publishing
Techno House, Redcliffe Way
Bristol (UK)
BS1 6NX
Fax +44 117 925 1942

Notation

A	Sabine absorption or equivalent absorption area: m^3
a	diameter of source: m
B	bending stiffness: Nm
c	wave speed: m/s
D	isolation (gross): dB
D_n	standard sound isolation: dB
d	distance: m
d	decay rate: dB/s
E	modulus of elasticity: N/m^2
F	force: N
f	frequency: s^{-1} or Hz
h	thickness: m
i	angle of incidence: rad
i	instantaneous intensity: W/m^2
I	average sound intensity: W/m^2
K	stiffness: N/m
LX	level of quantity X: dB
M	mass: kg
m	suffix (whole number)
P	pressure: N/m^2
P_0	atmospheric pressure: N/m^2 (or Pa)
p, p_a	instantaneous pressure, alternating variation: N/m^2 (or Pa)
p	suffix (whole number)
Q	directivity factor: dimensionless
Q	quality coefficient: dimensionless
r	suffix (whole number)

R	sound reduction index: dB
r	distance to a source: m
T	period: s
T	torque (Nm)
T_F	transmissibility (of force or of torque): dimensionless
T	thermodynamic temperature: K
T_R	reverberation time: s
t	time: s
t	energy transmission factor: dimensionless
V	volume: m^3
v	particle velocity: m/s
W	average sound power: W
w	instantaneous power: W
Z	mechanical impedance: Ns/m .
Z	acoustic impedance (per area unit): Ns/m^3

M	mega-: 10^6
k	kilo-: 10^3
m	milli-: 10^{-3}
μ	micro-: 10^{-6}
dB	decibel (dimensionless)
kg	kilogram
m	metre
N	newton
Pa	pascal: N/m^2
s	second
rad	radian
W	watt: J/s

α	Sabine absorption coefficient: dimensionless
δ	spring deflection: m
δ	static deviation, elastomer: m
δ	step difference (waves): m
δV	elementary volume: m^3
ε	relative damping rate: dimensionless
η	loss factor: dimensionless

NOTATION

θ	angle (emission or incident): rad
λ	wavelength: m
ρ	density: kg/m^3
σ	Poisson's ratio: dimensionless
σ	radiation factor: dimensionless

Index

absorption, *see* sound absorption
acceleration, in oscillatory
     movement 4
accelerometer 136
acoustic bitumen/tars 248, 251,
     252
acoustic bridges 97
acoustic tars 251, 252
active façades 267–273
active noise control 34
adaptive and active transmission
     149
airborne transmission 97–99,
     166–167
  insulation 247–249
  in roller shutters 235
  in tubular motors 197, 198, 199,
     200–201
  in window-shutter units
     204–205
alternating motion 6–10
alternating waves 27–29
aluminium
  density 247, 249–250
  projection screens 259
  vibration insulators
     249–251
  window-shutter units 205–208,
     257, 264
amplitude 6

anechoic rooms 82–84
antinodes 46, 49
attenuation 20, 29–31, 67–68
  in rooms 80–81
  through walls 88–96
awnings 217, 218–219, 236–241

beams (radiation)
  propagation 39–42
  reflection 68–69, 81
beams/tubes 197, 289
bearings 180
blinds
  exterior 214, 217–219, 236–241,
     249, 267–270
  sound pressure levels for 115
  venetian 208–210, 225–228, 258,
     261
braces/brackets 158–159, 160, 168,
     237–238, 239, 259
brain–ear system 60–61
brushes 249

casings
  lintel 215, 217, 234–236, 258
  motorized tube 152–155
  projection screen 164–168, 211–
     213, 259, 261
  roller shutter 248, 257, 260–261
  venetian blind 210, 258, 261